Vera Komissar

IN SPITE OF IT ALL

Julius Paltiel: A Norwegian Jew in Auschwitz

Vera Komissar

IN SPITE OF IT ALL

Julius Paltiel
A Norwegian Jew in Auschwitz

Translated from the Norwegian by Cheska Komissar

יד ושם
YAD VASHEM
THE WORLD HOLOCAUST REMEMBRANCE CENTER
THE INTERNATIONAL INSTITUTE FOR HOLOCAUST RESEARCH

Vera Komissar

På tross av alt

Julius Paltiel, norsk jøde i Auschwitz

Academic Editor: Therkel Stræde
Language and Production Editor: Adina Mendelsohn

P.O.B. 3477, Jerusalem 9103401, Israel
publications.marketing@yadvashem.org.il
First published in Norwegian by Aschehoug Forlag, 1995

ISBN: 978-965-308-674-6

Typesetting: Hava Salzman

Printed in Israel by Printiv Press, Jerusalem

*In memory of Kaja Paltiel, Idar Paltiel,
and the six million other innocent victims.*

CONTENTS

FOREWORD

A Road of Many Tears from Trondheim to Auschwitz to Buchenwald and Home: The Holocaust Memoirs of Julius Paltiel

ONE

> *Today there are only very few of us left to bear witness to the horrors of the German concentration camps. I feel that it is my duty to spread the knowledge of this tragedy. It is painful to remember. But it must be done.*

Robert Savosnick (1915–1998) wrote these words in the opening chapter of his book, published first in 1986 in his native Norwegian, and many years after his death in English and in German.[1] Savosnick, a medical student in 1942, felt an urge to give voice to the Norwegian Jews who had perished in Auschwitz and to

1 Robert Savosnick and Hans Melien, *Jeg ville ikke dø* (Cappelen: Oslo, 1986), 2nd ed. by Aktive Fredsforlag, Risør 2004); *I Did Not Want to Die. From Norway to Auschwitz* (Yad Vashem: Jerusalem, 2021); *Ich wollte nicht sterben. Als Norweger in Auschwitz* (Metropol: Berlin, 2021).

describe the road of suffering of the few survivors, a suffering that did not end with liberation. Today there are even fewer left who can give a living testimony, but fortunately, there are written texts left by survivors of the horrors, including the memoirs of Robert Savosnick and Julius Paltiel, both Norwegian Jews. Despite some commonality between their testimonies, it is in fact the differences between their accounts that portray the need to record each individual survivor testimony.

Norway had a very small Jewish population of only 2,000, but the Nazis extended their persecution to even the last Jews in the most remote areas of Europe. Half of the Norwegian Jews were able to make it through forests and snowdrifts to safety in Sweden, but 773 Jews were deported to the Auschwitz extermination camp; most of them were murdered in the gas chambers on the very day they arrived. Only able-bodied young and middle-aged men were assigned to forced labor in the Auschwitz concentration camp system under murderous conditions. Just thirty-eight of the Jewish deportees from Norway survived the Nazi camps—all men and most of them in their early twenties.

Julius Paltiel was one of them. Like Savosnick, Julius Louis Paltiel (1924–2008) grew up in Norway's third-largest city, Trondheim, located on the Atlantic shore halfway between the capital, Oslo, and the Arctic Circle. Paltiel participated in the life of the small Jewish community as well as in sports. He was eighteen when he was arrested by the Norwegian police of his native city in October 1942. The Savosnick and Paltiel families were both active in the textile and clothing business and knew each other from Trondheim's small Jewish community, but Robert and Julius followed different paths in life. Robert Savosnick studied medicine at the University of Oslo and was arrested while doing an internship near Trondheim. After the war, he became a renowned physician in his native city. Julius Paltiel helped with the family clothing store before the deportation and returned to working in the textile business after the war.

Their road from arrest to suffering in the Nazi camps and prisons on Norwegian and German soil are similar, but their stories are distinctly different. Both experienced the Falstad camp and Bredtveit prison from the inside. And, while German captivity in Norway was menacing for all and lethal for some, it was nothing compared to the more notorious Nazi concentration camps, as far as atrocities and deadly living conditions were concerned. Robert Savosnick and Julius Paltiel were deported by ship to Stettin (today, Szczecin in Poland), eventually arriving at Auschwitz-Birkenau a few days later. Both lined up for selection and were transferred to forced labor at the IG Farben Buna plant in nearby Monowitz, where a huge factory for synthetic rubber was being constructed.

They arrived in Monowitz with other Norwegian prisoners, but their paths took different directions. They were accommodated in primitive huts behind electrified barbed-wire fences and given miserable food, the nutritional value of which was far from sufficient to maintain the corporal strength of human beings who had to perform heavy construction work. Both ended up in the *Revier* (sick bay) as patients, but because of his medical background Savosnick was able to get a job as a medical orderly. This new position secured him lighter indoor work, but it exposed him to contagious diseases and close contact with vicious SS men and menacing prisoner functionaries. However, after Paltiel's recovery, he found himself back at the building site and subjected anew to hard labor under changing weather conditions and facing the random violence of SS guards as well as the reported violence of the Kapos. The menace of imminent death was everywhere in Auschwitz, but a medical orderly in the *Revier* had a greater chance of survival than those prisoners who had to do the dirty and dangerous construction work digging ditches and handling heavy cables, tubes, and steel modules without the necessary tools or safety equipment.

Both men saw friends from back home and camp comrades stumble and die. Already during the first months in the camp, the death toll among the deportees from Norway was frightening. When the Nazi concentration camp system expanded vastly during 1944, the prisoners who were transported to subcamps near and far lost the fragile protection that their knowledge of the Auschwitz routines had provided. While Savosnick was taken to a concentration camp in the ruins of what had once been the Warsaw ghetto until the uprising in 1943, Paltiel remained working at the Buna construction site as a prisoner of what was now known as Monowitz, a camp in itself with 12,000 prisoners, mostly Jewish. In mid-January 1945 he was in a group of more than

50,000 Auschwitz prisoners who were evacuated on foot to Gleiwitz and from there in open railway cars to Buchenwald. Arriving more dead than alive, and having seen many fellow prisoners die on the journey, he avoided a transport to a subcamp and thus spent the last months in the Buchenwald main camp, and the last days in the camp in a hideout provided by members of the Communist resistance of the camp. On April 11, 1945, he left the hideout to experience the liberation of what was one of the largest and deadliest camps in the Nazi concentration camp system.

Robert Savosnick, Herman Sachnowitz (1921–1978)—a merchant who was deported from Larvik in southern Norway to Monowitz and also wrote a book after the war about his time in Auschwitz[2]—and Julius Paltiel shared much of the same camp experience, but their paths before and after their captivity were different, and so was the way they talked about their recollections. Their Holocaust memoirs are valuable personal narratives, but they all found it difficult to get their impressions and reflections together in a narrative that would speak to others, so they required some assistance to write them down on paper. Savosnick was aided by journalist Hans Melien, and Sachnowitz was helped by prizewinning author and cartoonist Arnold Jacoby. Paltiel's memoirs were the result of countless conversations he had with his Danish–Jewish wife, Vera Komissar, a trained journalist, together with her careful editing. Each of these memoirs should be read in its own right. In spite of their similarities, they are quite different in detail as well as in diction, and each carries a strong, profound, and moving message to posterity.

For Julius Paltiel, the urge to testify to the injustice and cruelty of Nazism became a motive for surviving the camps, a purpose that helped him make it through the extremely difficult last months of the war. The threat of death was constantly hanging over the prisoners' heads in Monowitz, during the death march, and even more so in Buchenwald as his physical strength was deteriorating.

2 Herman Sachnowitz and Arnold Jacoby, *Det angår også deg* (Cappelen: Oslo, 1976).

TWO

The Jews of Norway were hit hard during the Holocaust. Close to half of the Jewish inhabitants of the country perished in Auschwitz, while a small number had already been killed in the Falstad concentration camp or elsewhere on Norwegian soil. Persecution by local Nazis, collaborationist Norwegian authorities, and the Germans split the small Jewish population in two. After a beginning, common to all, the two groups experienced the Holocaust very differently: one group faced uprooting, flight, rescue, and return, with difficulties along the way, experiencing the Holocaust "the Danish way," so to speak; for the other group the experience consisted of sudden arrest, deportation, forced labor, death, and the return of only a tiny fragment, akin to the experience of the Polish Jews. Common to both was the fact that spoliation—the confiscation of Jewish property by the Norwegian state—was an integral part of the process, something that victimized both the refugees and those who were murdered, and made the return of the survivors to Norway after the war difficult and painful.

A few Jews from Norway made it to Britain, and 925 were able to flee with the help of local non-Jews through sparsely populated forest areas to the border of neutral Sweden. The Swedish authorities, concerned about their lucrative trade relations and general cooperation with Nazi Germany, and reflecting the antisemitism that was widespread in parts of Swedish society, turned away some of the first Jewish refugees, but eventually changed their minds and welcomed Jewish refugees, as was the case with the far larger number of resistance fighters and their family members fleeing persecution and hostage-taking by the Germans and local Nazis in Norway.[3]

3 See Karin Kvist Geverts, *Ett främmande element i nationen. Svensk flyktingpolitik og de judiska flyktingerna 1938–1944* (Acta Universitatis Uppsaliensis Nr. 233: Uppsala, 2007).

THREE

The presence of Jews in Norway followed later than other countries. During the centuries of Danish reign (1500–1800), Jews found their way from Denmark to Norway in small numbers. However, after Norway gained autonomy, its first constitution adopted at the Eidsvoll mansion in 1814 included a ban on Jews and Jesuits, who were not allowed to set foot on the soil of the strongly evangelical country for half a decade. Even Jews who were shipwrecked and made it to the Norwegian shore were jailed and punished for violating the ban. Only when the decree was lifted in 1851 did Jews begin to settle in Norwegian cities, towns, and hamlets as businessmen, small traders, and urban professionals. The establishment of Jewish communal life with philanthropical and burial societies, schooling for children, and the first synagogue opening in 1892 in the capital Kristiania (today, Oslo), portrays a prosperous community that was able to get the means together for a full-fledged Jewish infrastructure in spite of its small numbers.

The country's second synagogue opened in 1925 in Trondheim, where a former railway station had been refurbished to serve as the spiritual center of Jewish life in the mid-Norwegian region of Trøndelag. This is the synagogue the Paltiel family frequented, and where young Julius had his bar mitzvah in 1937.

Many Jews who immigrated to Norway came from Denmark and Sweden, but the Jews from these neighboring countries were soon followed by others from the lands of the Russian tsar seeking refuge in Norway from pogroms and poverty in their homelands. Soon after, as Hitler came to power in Germany and made the persecution of Jews a state policy, refugees started coming in from Germany (from 1933), Austria (from 1938), and occupied, dismembered Czechoslovakia (from 1939). The ruling Labor Party welcomed political refugees like the future West German chancellor Willy Brandt and sexual reformer Wilhelm Reich, but failed to recognize that Jews were political victims of Nazism until the "*Kristallnacht*" pogrom on November 9, 1938, demonstrated the murderous character of Nazi persecution to the world.

Norwegian authorities did their utmost to keep Jewish refugees away, so only 350 were living in the country on April 9, 1940, when the German forces invaded Norway and eventually forced the king and government into exile in Great Britain.

If Norwegian nationalism had been strong before, the foreign occupation fortified a strong sense of identity in many Norwegians who wanted to continue fighting the Germans even after the military confrontations had ceased. A clandestine resistance movement emerged early on. However, a significant minority of Norwegians sided with the occupying power, and opted for economic and administrative collaboration, as well as the adoption of Nazi ideology, which catered to the excessive nationalism of the Norwegians by courting Norwegians as the representatives of the "Aryan" master race.

Norwegian Nazis had the backing of some 10 percent of the population, and this enabled them to take over leading positions in the police, central and local administration, and eventually to take over the government. In 1942, the occupying power made Norwegian Nazi leader Vidkun Quisling prime minister. He had unsuccessfully attempted a coup d'état in 1940, and the fact that he was able to stay in power until the German capitulation of May 8, 1945, speaks volumes about the backing he had in parts of Norwegian society and among the elites. The antisemitic utterances by him and his followers along with the anti-Jewish laws were not without support in parts of Norwegian society, in spite of the fact that the Jewish minority, totaling only 2,000, equaled less than 1 percent of the country's 3 million inhabitants. However, Jews were very present as an enemy image in the teachings of some of the competing evangelical sects that had a strong position in Norway, particularly in the sparsely populated rural areas. Whereas Danish Jews felt that they could rely on the general population—the majority of whom grew up with a philosemitic brand of Lutheran Christianity—for help and support, and the rescue operation of the Danish Jews in October 1943 proved them right, the Jews of Norway had to face the fact that significant parts of society would turn against them, not least the police and the civil service.

FOUR

In Norway, some Jews were arrested early on, and a few were deported to German camps because they were believed to have connections to the resistance movement. Then, from November 1942, after rounds of arrest, 737 Jews were deported in four transports on German ships from the harbor of Oslo: twenty-one Jews on the SS *Monte Rosa* on November 20 and twenty-six Jews on November 26; 532 Jews on the SS *Donau* on November 26; and 158 Jews on the SS *Gotenland* on February 24, 1943.[4]

The German occupying authorities did not have to do much to encourage the Norwegian Nazis of Vidkun Quisling's National Unity party (Nasjonal Samling, NS) to start persecuting the country's Jewish minority. Discriminatory laws and regulations aimed at segregation were issued in quick succession including registration, the introduction of a "J" stamped on Jewish identity papers, vicious antisemitic propaganda and harassment, and the registration and confiscation of property. During 1942, selected male Jews were arrested and sentenced to forced labor under brutal conditions, followed by all male Jews above the age of fifteen on October 26, 1942. The deportation of those who had not been able to flee the country, now also including Jewish women and children, followed from November 1942.

FIVE

The deportees' journey from Norway ended in Auschwitz where, from March 1942, the Nazi program of total physical annihilation was running at high speed with Jews arriving on transports from all over

4 Earlier information about numbers and other details have been corrected by later research; see Bjarte Bruland, ed., *Øyenvitner. Rapport etter norske jøders hjemkomst fra koncentrationsleirene* (Dinamo: Oslo, 2012) p.15ff.; and HL-Senteret, *Deportasjonen av de norske jødene,* https://www.hlsenteret.no/kunnskapsbasen/folkemord/folkemord-under-nazismen/holocaust/norge/deportasjonen-av-de-norske-jodene.html (2017). Some uncertainty still exists.

German–occupied Europe. As is well known today, the majority were killed by Zyklon B in the gas chambers of Birkenau immediately upon arrival. Only a minority of Jews, considered particularly strong and "able-bodied" by the SS, were selected to enter the Auschwitz camp complex as prisoners, destined to perform exhausting forced labor in the vast workshops, factories, and construction projects that belonged to the largest and most lethal of all Nazi concentration camps.

The proportion of Norwegian Jews who were selected for forced labor, as opposed to being sent directly to the gas chambers, was higher than average for Auschwitz. Of the Jews from the SS *Donau*, over 35 percent—a total of 186 Jews, all men—became prisoners of Auschwitz. The SS was in acute need of forced laborers to work in camp maintenance and at the building site in nearby Monowitz where IG Farben—then Europe's largest chemical corporation—was constructing a huge plant for the production of so-called Buna (synthetic rubber).

SIX

Julius Paltiel was one of 120 Norwegian Jews from his transport who was sent to what was at the time called Auschwitz III—Monowitz camp. Here, he and the others were put to hard unskilled labor at the Buna factory construction site. Thousands of prisoners from all over Europe provided the successful corporation with cheap labor. Some would become famous as witnesses after the Holocaust, like Imre Kertész and Elie Wiesel from Hungary and the Italian Primo Levi.

The prisoners were given nothing but inadequate portions of substandard food in return for long working days. Very soon, the first of the Norwegians succumbed to the hardship and hunger. A concentration camp inmate could expect to live some three to nine months, but even less at Buna due to the heavy labor and the excessive violence of the guards and Kapos. Death certificates of some of the Norwegian Jews, preserved in the Auschwitz-Birkenau State Museum archive, confirm that the Norwegian prisoners died at an even faster rate than most prisoners, although they had been healthy and well nourished when they arrived; most lasted only two to three months under the extreme conditions of the Monowitz camp.[5] Paltiel, young and sturdy, who also reached the point of near-breakdown, was allowed into a sickbed, recovered, and made it through months of deprivation. At one point he was subjected to brutal torture by the camp Gestapo. He even survived the death march to Gleiwitz and the transport to Buchenwald, which cost the lives of some 10,000–15,000 prisoners out of 58,000.

SEVEN

Knowledge of the deadly conditions in the Nazi concentration camps was widespread in Scandinavia already before the liberation of Majdanek on July 22, 1944, which disclosed the horrors to representatives of the free world. BBC radio news was referenced in Swedish newspapers as well as in the illegal press of Denmark and Norway. Reacting to initiatives by the Norwegian exile in Sweden, the Danish authorities put pressure on the Germans for permission to repatriate the Scandinavian deportees from German camps and prisons. At the same time, they discreetly built up an evacuation organization that succeeded in bringing the first of 25,000 prisoners back to Denmark in December 1944, and eventually all Scandinavians plus thousands of other prisoners.

In Copenhagen, on his way back to Norway after the liberation, Paltiel actually met one of the initiators of the rescue operation, Borghild Hammerich. As the Swedes joined the operation in February 1945, SS leader Heinrich Himmler—hoping to get on good negotiating terms with the Western Allies and convince them to join forces with Nazi Germany against the Soviet Union—agreed to evacuate all Scandinavians to Sweden, provided the Scandinavians took care of the logistics. Convoys of "White Buses" with Red Cross symbols started bringing Danes and Norwegians back from camps and prisons spread out across the entire German Reich.

5 Results of an investigation, carried out by the author and history students from the University of Southern Denmark (Odense) in the Auschwitz–Birkenau State Museum archive in May 2014.

Danish evacuation functionaries went to great lengths in order to reach the remainder of the 470 Jews who had been deported from Denmark in 1943–1944 to the ghetto of Theresienstadt near Prague and bring them safely back. The few Norwegian survivors of Auschwitz encountered anti-Jewish sentiment among Norwegian evacuation functionaries and disinterest among the majority of the Norwegian *KZ-Häftlinge* (concentration camp prisoners) who were deemed Aryan by the Nazis: Robert Savosnick was deeply disillusioned when he was left behind in the Dachau subcamp of Allach near Munich and could only return to Norway much later. Similarly, Julius Paltiel experienced being left behind by the "White Buses" as his Aryan fellow prisoners were driven to safety in Sweden.

During the many months in the hell of the camps, both men had cherished the love of Norway and "Norwegian values" more than any Jewish symbols. But in the very moment of liberation, Norwegian functionaries and fellow sufferers let them understand that, like the German Nazis, they too considered the Jews as aliens, as if they were not citizens of Norway, and felt no solidarity with them. Both Savosnick and Paltiel recall the blow; neither of them ever overcame the bitterness they felt by being left behind by their fellow Norweigians.[6]

EIGHT

In spite of this discouraging experience, in late May 1945, Julius Paltiel was euphoric as he finally set foot on Norwegian soil again: "Norway, Norway, it sings inside of me. My legs move lightly down the ladder and onto the dock." Despite having been arrested and put through the first of many torments by Norwegian police, sent through a life-threatening journey through the death camps on Norwegian order, and having been left behind by Norwegian prisoners who were eager to return home and cared nothing about their Jewish co-sufferers, Norwegian nationalism made his heart swell as he returns.

6 Savosnick, *I Did Not Want to Die*, p. 193.

Upon the return of Paltiel and four other Auschwitz survivors, only three resistance fighters—friends of one of the survivors—a Red Cross representative, and Naftali Hirsch, a young Jew who had survived in hiding in Norway, are there to greet them. The engraving of the silver cup, decorated with Norwegian flags, that Hirsch presented as a homecoming gift, symbolizes the marginalization of the Jews that was characteristic in German-occupied Norway, and in Norwegian postwar memory for many years: "Buchenwald 1942–1945. Welcome to Norway. May 1945. Naftali Hirsch." Buchenwald was a place of suffering for non-Jewish Norwegians, and only briefly for a handful of Norwegian Jews during the very last stages of the war. Their place of torment and death throughout 1942–1945 had been Auschwitz.

NINE

The description of Julius Paltiel's first months back in liberated Norway—his loneliness despite help from understanding friends, his doubts and confusion about the future—is just as strong as his depictions of the atrocities and the misery he encountered during his time in captivity. He finally decided to mend whatever could be mended: to start from the bottom and get the family clothing store up and running again, even though the family was no longer there. And he engaged himself in seeking justice, participated as a witness in war crimes trials against some of Norway's worst perpetrators, and engaged himself in the fight against antisemitism. At the end of the book, we see him at a survivors' reunion in Jerusalem. He leaves it to another survivor to say the final words: "Don't tell us it never happened. We were there.... We are the living witnesses and we will continue to speak out until the last survivor is no more."[7]

7 Sam E. Bloch, ed., *From Holocaust to Redemption: Bearing Witness. A documentary volume depicting the proceedings and events of the World Gathering of Jewish Holocaust Survivors, Israel, June 1981* (New York: The World Gathering of Jewish Holocaust Survivors, 1984), p. 50.

When living witnesses are no longer here to help later generations understand what happened when a part of the world—governments and civil society—turned against the small and powerless Jewish minority, fortunately we will still have books, written testimonies like that of Julius Paltiel, a young, and in many respects, quite ordinary Jew, a survivor from the fringe of Europe during the Holocaust.

Therkel Stræde

INTRODUCTION

Sunbeams flash like lightning before my eyes. My head explodes. I kick the man's rear end. An uncontrollable kick against the hated enemy. He falls. Friendly hands grab me, accompanied with calming words. The moment is over.

We are a small band of men gathered in the Falstad forest watching the SS dig up graves they have filled with victims of war. The man I kicked into the grave was the former commander of the German security police of central Norway, Gerhard Friedrich Ernst Flesch.[1] Now he has stood up again and continues to dig up the corpses of people he had ordered to be killed. The Falstad forest is dense and the sun is barely able to penetrate the thick undergrowth on that late summer day in August 1945. The light makes the forest appear bewitched.

The inhumanity of the war is only a few months past: Three months ago, I came home from the hell of the concentration camps. On orders from Reichskommissar Josef Terboven,[2] it was Flesch who

1 *SS-Obersturmbannführer* Gerhard Friedrich Ernst Flesch (1909–1948), a lawyer by training, commanded an Einsatzkommando that took part in the German assault on Poland in 1939. He was appointed commander of the Sicherheitsdienst (the German Security Police) in Bergen in 1940, and subsequently in Trondheim from October 1941 to May 1945. He was executed as a war criminal.

2 Josef Antonius Heinrich Terboven (1898–1945) was an early member of the

ordered that my people and I should be arrested and sent to Germany. It was Flesch who ordered the arrest of all the Jews in Trondheim, starting with the arrest of all male Jews over the age of fifteen on October 7, 1942, followed by the women, who were interned in three apartments in the city from October 7 to November 25, before they too were arrested. It was Flesch who was responsible for the torture and murder of ordinary people and prisoners in Falstad concentration camp. I have kicked him so that he feels the earth in his face. That wet, sticky, moldy earth of the Falstad forest. It gives me a good feeling. Now I am totally calm.

I am present as a witness, to help identify these innocent people who lie here without coffins. People that did not receive a burial or memorial. Now they will be able to move to the cemetery where they belong and lie where their loved ones wish them to receive their final resting place.

The night grows long. I can't sleep. I wander restless around the apartment. The windows are wide open, lest I don't get enough air. I am lonesome. Alone. The pictures I see in my mind's eye will not release me. Everything is so fresh.

Again, I feel the pain that overwhelmed me when Pappa[3] died. I was eleven years old. It was the day after Christmas in 1935 and Pappa was in the cabin in Bymarka, a recreation area in the city, putting shutters on the windows. He wanted to hurry home. He and Mamma were going to a birthday party at their best friend's, John Fjeldvik,[4] so

German Nazi party (the NSDAP) and Gauleiter of Essen, an industrial center in the Ruhr area where his SA gangs fought the strong labor movement. From 1940 to 1945 he was Reichskommissar in occupied Norway. He was the top Nazi official, and became a symbol of Nazi oppression and atrocities. He killed himself on the day of Germany's capitulation on May 9, 1945.

3 Salomon Paltiel (1889–1935) was born in Lund, Sweden, and came to Trondheim as a young child when his father, Israel Moses Paltiel (1852–1918), founded what became a successful clothing shop in the central Norwegian city. The small family lived in the first-floor apartment of the same building on Brattørgaten, and Julius's mother, Kaja Ruth, née Friedländer (1895–1943), ran the store with the help of Julius and his older brother, Idar Israel (1919–1943).

4 John Fjeldvik (1888–1961), a Trondheim stockbroker.

he ran to catch the trolley to Gråkall. He boarded the trolley, greeted several acquaintances with "Merry Christmas," took a seat, and died of a stroke that same moment. I couldn't understand it. He was with us and then he wasn't anymore. My dear father. He was forty-six years old. My mother was forty-one.

Poor Mamma. At that time, I could not understand her dark sorrow and loneliness. I viewed it as **my** grief. Now Mamma and my innocent older brother, Idar, are also gone. The tears stream down my face. The day's experiences in the Falstad forest play over and over again. Finally, sleep comes.

PART ONE

CAPTURED

ONE

I hear the doorbell ring at the crack of dawn. I am half asleep. It is Wednesday morning. I open the door. Two men in dark-blue uniforms stand outside, their gold buttons glimmer. These are Norwegian police sergeants, with regulation hats on their heads. They ask after Idar and Julius Paltiel. I tell them that I am Julius Paltiel and ask what this is about. They inform me that I am under arrest. Now, I am wide awake.

The previous evening, police officer Alfred Geving,[5] a frequent customer, came to the store to warn me that all Jewish males over fifteen years old will be arrested tonight and that I must go into hiding. Geving asked me if I had a place to go where I could vanish and I told him that I did. I thanked him for the message, and he disappeared in the fall darkness. That night I went into hiding and stayed with a neighbor. With a threat to his own life, Alfred Geving had come to our door and

5 Engvald Alfred Jule Geving (1902–1979) was a police officer in Trondheim.

told us that he had seen typed lists with the names of all the Jews that would be arrested on the night between October 6 and 7, 1942.

Martial law is implemented on October 6 in Trondheim. Leading an SS delegation are Reichskommissar Josef Terboven and *SS-Obergruppenführer* and General der Polizei, Wilhelm Rediess,[6] who came to town one month earlier following acts of sabotage near Lake Majavatn. Two German soldiers were killed. These two prominent representatives for the occupying power gave inflammatory speeches in the center of Trondheim, warning against civil disobedience, and promising revenge. And revenge is not late in coming.

Hardworking, conscientious employees at the police station in Hornemannsgården ensured that lists of names of the city's Jewish men were collected. Police officer Alfred Geving defied the ban against leaking information about these lists. I was warned a little before 8:00 P.M. on Tuesday evening. But where should I go so close to curfew coming into effect? Mamma and I agreed that I would stay at the neighbors that first night, and run away the next day. I sat on the neighbors' recliner in a half-sleep the entire night. I was in an unfamiliar living room, with a gray sofa, wine-red curtains, and the obligatory blackout blinds pulled down. Throughout my light sleep, I strained to hear if a car had stopped outside, on my street, Brattørgaten, a car that was supposed to be for me. What would I do with myself when the new day arrived? Who could I trust? How would I get to Sweden? Such thoughts plagued me that night in the recliner.

In the previous months, I had begged and implored Mamma hundreds of times to flee with me. But each time she answered that she would not flee, that she has not done anything wrong. She believed

6 Friedrich Wilhelm Otto Rediess (1900–1945), *SS-Obergruppenführer* and Police General. He was the Higher SS and Police leader of East Prussia from 1940 until 1945 and he was also the Higher SS and Police leader of Norway. Located in Oslo, Rediess was responsible for some of the first deportations of Jews after the German occupation of Poland and for the "Sonderkommando Lange" murders of handicapped and psychiatric patients in mobile gas chambers. In Norway, he was in charge of fighting the resistance and of implementing the Lebensborn program of multiplying the "Aryan" "Nordic" race in Norway. He killed himself on May 8, 1945, the day of Germany's capitulation.

that no one would do any harm to an aging woman like her and so she would stay. I was eighteen years old and I was not able to convince Mamma that we ought to flee. My arguments didn't have any influence. At the same time, I was not able to leave her. I was afraid of how the Germans would punish Mamma. Regarding my twenty-three-year-old brother, Idar, he has been sick with rheumatic fever for some time and has been convalescing at the farm of his fiancée, Maja (Marie) Sachnowitz,[7] near Larvik.

"Under arrest?"

Both police sergeants nod. It has only been an hour since I returned to our apartment after the previous night's stay in the neighbors' living room. It is barely six o'clock and the gray October light just filters through the window. When the curfew was lifted at five o'clock, I thought the danger was over. The police sergeants' incessant ringing of the doorbell had forced me out of bed. I thought I would be able to get a few hours' sleep before I had to run.

Thoughts fly through my head. How am I going to run away from these two police sergeants? Escape on the way up the stairs? Or out the back door? But the sergeants follow me like shadows into the apartment. Mamma sits in the living room. She had woken as suddenly as I had. A cold gust of wind enters the warm, familiar living room along with the two uniformed men.

The orders to take toiletries and some warm clothing are clear. I am followed into my room. I throw some warm clothes in the backpack that is already out in preparation for my escape. A ski sweater, socks, and mittens lie on the table.

I am not able to speak with Mamma alone. Not even for a moment. I so much want to tell her that she must leave here immediately. But Mamma will not understand. She doesn't want to leave her home, the

7 Maja (Marie) Sachnowitz (1919–1942) was an amateur singer and musician. She worked as a waitress and was also a beauty queen in her native Larvik. She was arrested on November 26, 1942, and deported aboard the SS *Donau* with her father, five brothers, and fiancé, Idar Paltiel. She was murdered upon arrival in Auschwitz-Birkenau.

only safe place she knows. I can see that she is worried about what will happen to her son, and she's thinking about what's happening in Larvik, about Idar. Hopefully he is safe. We haven't dared to ask about much on the telephone, and now it's impossible to contact him. Eventually, I tell her to take care of herself. I give her a quick hug. As the policemen lead me out of the apartment, I think to myself how small she looks.

Out on the street, I turn to look at the building with the redbrick facade. Over the store window I see the sign, S. Paltiel. Men's Clothing. Est. 1891. I get into the car. Almost three years will pass before I see my home again.

Julius Paltiel in the summer of 1940. Courtesy of the Jewish Museum, Trondheim.

Idar and Julius Paltiel. Courtesy of the Jewish Museum, Trondheim.

Salomon Paltiel and shop assistant, Åsa Lagerquist outside the S. Paltiel store. Courtesy of the Jewish Museum, Trondheim.

TWO

The car stops outside the jail on Kongens gate (King Street). I am thrown into a cell with so many Jewish men. I know them all. One of the oldest men there is my dear uncle, Aron Mendelsohn.[8] He is over seventy years old. My guardian and eldest cousin Henrik Mendelsohn[9] is also there. These two people helped me so much after my father died.

I am the youngest in the cell, having just turned eighteen. We stand together and look at one another. Each of us is filled with hundreds of unanswered questions. We've obviously heard what has happened to the Jews in Germany, but we never would have believed it could happen here at home. Norway has approximately 2,000 Jewish residents. About 900 of them live in Oslo, the rest mostly in Trondheim, Kristiansund, and northern Norway. In the past few years, about 400 German, Austrian, and Czech Jews have immigrated to Norway—but we still number so few. Some Jews had predicted what would happen and they fled to Sweden. We did not believe that a mass arrest of Jews was possible in Norway.

That evening we are driven further up the street to Vollan prison, across from the circular-shaped building of the Student Society

8 Aron Miche Mendelsohn (1871–1943) was born in Lithuania. He moved to Trondheim in 1894 where he married Thora Paltiel in the first Jewish wedding ever in the city. Starting his career as a traveling salesman, he worked his way up to founding a successful retail store, A. Mendelsohn & Sønner, and the clothing factory, Trondhjems Konfektionsfabrik. A prominent member of the Trondheim Jewish community, he was arrested on November 7, 1942, and initially taken to the Falstad internment camp. He was later sent to the Bredtveit prison in Oslo. On February 24, 1943, he was deported with his wife on the SS *Gotenland* to Auschwitz-Birkenau where he and Thora were murdered upon arrival.

9 Henrik Mendelsohn (1896–?) was the eldest son of Aron and Thora Mendelsohn. He had taken over his father's clothing store, A. Mendelsohn & Sønner. On November 7, 1942, he was arrested and taken to the Falstad internment camp. His business was confiscated by the Norwegian state. Later he was taken to the Bredtveit prison in Oslo, and on February 24, 1943, he was deported on the SS *Gotenland* to Auschwitz-Birkenau where he was selected for forced labor. He died in the Auschwitz III–Monowitz camp. His date of death is unknown.

in Trondheim. It is here where we spend our first night as prisoners. Prisoners in Trondheim! We sleep little that night, all thinking of our loved ones. At the crack of dawn, before darkness releases its hold, we are woken up. We will be transferred to Falstad prison camp near Levanger. I am one of twenty-seven men who are transported to the Trondheim train station by the Norwegian police. Together with us are seventy non-Jewish detainees.

The train stops at Ronglan Station, 8 kilometers from Ekne, where Falstad camp lies. The small area around the station is overflowing with German SS soldiers. Here is where they take over command. In tight, green uniforms and shiny black boots, they stand in rank to receive a new load of prisoners. The soldiers are rested, ready to show that they have complete control and that we are nothing but prisoners.

"*Los, los, aufstehen!* Don't stand there like a bunch of idiots! Line up, three per row."

Everything is yelled in German. It is the first time we are given orders in that language. The foreign language and the violent sounds confuse us as we are chased out of the train cars. It takes some time before we understand everything that is being yelled at us.

"Three in a row!" The Germans scream hysterically again and again.

"*Los! Schneller!* (Faster!)"

Finally, we stand, ready to go.

THREE

"March! Double time! One, two, three."

Many aren't physically fit and they are not able to run quickly with the backpacks or little suitcases they carry. The clothes we are wearing aren't very practical in the miserable gray rain that lies thick and heavy over the countryside. The naked tree trunks stand as if at attention for us. It's not long before we are soaked to the skin. But we hardly notice. Everyone is consumed with their own deep thoughts. I think about Mamma, who is alone in the city. Better she is spared from this. She still has her friends and Aunt Thora Mendelsohn[10] to support her, but both Idar and I are gone. I know she is worried, just as other women would worry about their husbands and sons under such terrible conditions. Has Mamma understood she, herself, must hide? I doubt it.

It is a mixed group of sad-looking men who are jogging toward Ekne. Our bodies are heavy with wet clothes and our small suitcases or backpacks are becoming heavier with each step. Thirst and hunger begin to torment us. The older go slower and slower, while the soldiers yell at us to go faster. The sky begins to darken as we march through the gate of the camp. It's October 1942. Over the gate hang the words, *Arbeit macht frei* (Work sets you free).

FOUR

Falstad lies in the center of the village of Ekne, about 10 kilometers south of Levanger in Nord-Trøndelag. Trondheim's Prison Authority purchased the farm in 1891 and in 1910, it was taken over by the state for use as a foster home for neglected boys. The main building was constructed of brick in 1921. In 1941, the German forces took over the area to use as a center for the Lebensborn program. But the Germans soon found Falstad more useful as a *Polizeihaftlager* (political prison). Falstad camp falls under Section IV of the Sicherheitsdienst (SD), which is part of the Geheime Staatspolizei (Gestapo). Everyone who works here is part of the German security police. German law rules here—justice, judgments, and decisions are at the mercy of the Gestapo. As soon as the Germans took over Falstad, a barbed-wire fence was erected around the perimeter. Prisoner barracks, guard towers, and firing posts were built. A sawmill, a carpentry shop, and a pig farm were set up within the barbed-wire fence. The prisoners would work here.

10 Thora Mendelsohn, née Paltiel (1874–1943) was born in Malmö, Sweden. At twenty, she moved to Trondheim where she met and married Aron Mendelsohn. Thora ran a shop in Trondheim and gave birth to nine children. On November 25, 1942, she was arrested and spent three months in the Bredtveit prison in Oslo. In spite of her claim to be a Swedish citizen, she was deported on the SS *Gotenland* in February 1943 to Auschwitz-Birkenau where she was murdered upon arrival.

From 1941, the Gestapo chief in Trondheim was Gerhard Friedrich Ernst Flesch. He reported to the police general Wilheim Rediess, who in turn reported directly to Reichskommissar Josef Terboven. Flesch was the leader of the Einsatzkommando deployed in Central Norway, which had its headquarters in the Misjonshotell in Trondheim. He was educated as a lawyer, he had been a member of the NSDAP (the official Nazi party) since 1933, and eventually joined the SS. Among other places, they sent him to the Sudetenland (a part of Czechoslovakia annexed by the Germans) and Poland. Terboven had brought Flesch with him to Norway in April 1940, and on October 11 the following year, Flesch was given responsibility for central Norway. One could not find a worse SS man in Norway. He worked closely with the informer and Norwegian torturer, Henry Oliver Rinnan,[11] and he himself participated in the torture of prisoners. Being the Nazi and antisemite that he was, Flesch had written a treatise on the inferiority of the Jews. At Falstad, he gave orders that Jews must not receive treatment in the infirmary, even in cases of serious illness. It was Flesch who stood behind the inhumane treatment that many prisoners experienced in Falstad. Supposedly, he said that as far as he is concerned, blood can flow every day in Falstad and one may gladly take the life of a Jew daily.

Falstad[12] was the Gestapo's most important camp in central Norway. Between 5,000 and 7,000 Norwegians were interned there from

11 *SS-Untersturmführer* Henry Oliver Rinnan (1915–1947) was a Norwegian Gestapo agent who led the Sonderabteilung Lola—known by Norwegians as Rinnanbanden (The Rinnan Gang)—which operated in the Trondheim area and was notorious for infiltrating resistance groups and torturing their victims. Of the many crimes committed by the gang, Rinnan was sentenced for thirteen murders and was executed in February 1947.

12 Falstad was originally a Christian boarding school and correctional facility for "misguided children" in the Trondheim district. From September 1941, it was used by the Germans as a prison camp and execution site. A minimum of 4,200 (mainly political) prisoners passed through Falstad. Most were taken to Grini, the largest German internment camp in Norway, or prisons in the Oslo area. Forty-seven male Jews from the Trondheim area were interned in Falstad and at least eight of them were murdered. The remainder were transported to Auschwitz via Oslo.

1941 until the end of the war. Some were there for just a short time, while others remained in the camp until May 1945. Falstad was also used as a transit camp for Norwegian Jews for a short period. Many Russian and Yugoslav prisoners of war were also incarcerated there. Falstad was an internment camp, a concentration camp, and a death camp.

Several hundred meters south of the camp lies the Falstad forest where over 200 prisoners—Norwegians, Russians, and Yugoslavs—were buried over the course of these years. The Germans used prisoners like the Serbian, Ljuban Vuković,[13] and the Russians, Alexander and Misja, as permanent gravediggers. Ljuban was particularly big and strong and never hesitated to demonstrate his enormous strength while doing this work. The SS used him as an example for other prisoners to follow and while he survived, many other prisoners died from exhaustion. They were not able to keep the same pace as the giant. Of these three gravediggers, only Ljuban survived.

Ten detainees from the Trondheim area who were killed during German martial law on October 7, 1942, were among the first to be temporarily laid to rest there. They were all prominent men: lawyer, Otto Skirstad;[14] theater manager, Henry Gleditsch;[15] editor, Harald Langhelle;[16] businessman, Hirsch Komissar;[17] engineer, Hans Konrad

13 Ljuban Vuković (1914–1987) was a Serbian prisoner of war who was brought to the Falstad camp on June 24, 1942. He was ordered to work as a gravedigger. During the last days of the war, the Germans apparently wanted to kill him in order to cover up evidence regarding the extent of the killings, but he managed to hide. He became an important witness in the postwar trials and in the efforts to identify the corpses of the Falstad victims.

14 Otto Benjamin Andreas Skirstad (1882–1942), an influential lawyer and conservative politician.

15 Henry Cochrane Williamsen Gleditsch (1902–1942), actor and director of the Trøndelag Teater in Trondheim.

16 Harald Langhelle (1890–1942), labor politician and editor of Trondheim's socialist newspaper *Arbeiter-Avisen*.

17 Hirsch Zvi Komissar (1887–1942), a Jewish businessman born in Belarus and educated in Germany as a machine engineer. He ran the Trondheim Paris-Wien fashion store and engaged in Zionist organizational work.

Ekornes;[18] banker, Gunnar Sandberg Birch;[19] shipping merchant, Per T. Lykke;[20] Captain Finn Berg;[21] lawyer, Gunnar Bull Aakrann[22] from Røros; and construction engineer, Peder Eggen[23] from Orkanger. They were neither put on trial nor convicted. Before the end of the war, the Germans dumped many of the dead in the Trondheim Fjord, probably so that future generations would not uncover the terrible mistreatment that the prisoners had experienced.

FIVE

The first thing I notice is the tall watchtowers next to the gate and the large, dark building that appears closed and unfriendly. Its silhouette stands heavy and looming in the late afternoon light. Only members of the German security police are around us. The silence is broken by the Germans' endless barking of orders and the sky's crying rain. The voices of the prisoners are broken. Yesterday's shooting of the ten detainees has made an unforgettable impression. Two of the prisoners,

18 Hans Konrad Ekornes (1911–1942), a second lieutenant of the Royal Norwegian Engineers working as construction site manager. He was a member of the Englandsfarten resistance group, which organized illegal transports by ship between Norway and the UK.

19 Gunnar Sandberg Birch (1894–1942) was the CEO of Forretningsbanken, a leading bank in northern Norway, and an active member of the resistance.

20 Per Tangen Lykke (1895–1942) was a leading businessman in Trondheim, involved in shipping and fur farming. He was known to the Germans for his resistance to the Nazification of Norwegian businesses.

21 Finn Berg (1897–1942) was an army captain who fought the Germans during the invasion of 1940 and became head of security at the Trondhjems Mekaniske Værksted, one of Norway's largest shipyards. He was also a member of the Milorg military resistance organization.

22 Gunnar Bull Aakrann (1899–1942) was a lawyer in Røros, a regional center 100 kilometers southeast of Trondheim. An anti-Nazi, he engaged himself in aiding refugees and couriers across the nearby border to Sweden.

23 Peder Eggen (1889–1942), a construction manager in charge of railroad repairs south of Trondheim. He was targeted by local Nazis and accused of slowing down work.

Hans Ekornes and Hirsch Komissar, were taken directly from their cells here in Falstad and killed. Who would be the next? This unspoken thought hovers over the prisoners.

A special commando of SS soldiers had come to Falstad to carry out the murders. Big, strong men who are trained to kill without asking why. On the same day, *SS-Obersturmbannführer* Flesch, together with other SS officers, conducted a court-martial for twenty-seven other men from the coast of Helgeland. These men were arrested and held after the acts of sabotage near Majavatn. One after the other they received their death sentence. That same day, in his customary style, Flesch gave an inflammatory speech to the prisoners in the yard. For the remainder of the day, the twenty-seven men awaited their inevitable fate. They weren't allowed to work. To wait is excruciating. It's better to have something into which to sink your fingers. Standing on a truck, they were transported to the Falstad forest. Ljuban, Alexander, and Misja had prepared a communal grave ahead of time. Twenty-seven men were lined up on the edge of the open grave. One after the other they were shot, liquidated.

We, the new prisoners, with our hopelessness, come trampling into this depressing situation. Our few belongings are soon taken from us—clothes, watches, money, pens, rings, pictures of our loved ones; everything is confiscated. We are allowed to keep only our toiletries. At the same time, we find out that all Jewish property has been seized. We feel naked in a double sense when our own clothes are replaced with gray prisoner clothing. The Jews are assigned a piece of white fabric cut out like a Star of David that we must sew on our prison clothes. That way the SS will be able to identify us easily. From now on, we are Jews, and only that. We are Jews.

All prisoners, including the Jews, have their hair cut, but we Jews are not allowed to cut our beards. We should not look like the others. We should feel different. We are not allowed to share barracks with other prisoners. We must sleep in the attic. There are no windows there, just small vents. The other prisoners are allowed to lie on cots in the barracks. We must lie on straw mattresses, on the floor. Yesterday, we Norwegians were among equals. Today we are twenty-seven Norwegian Jews separated from society.

Falstad is built like an atrium, with buildings on all four sides. From the outside it is impossible to see in. From the outside, no one can see what happens in the yard. All prisoners must stand upright and in line while the Germans count us. SS soldiers register each and every movement. If one of us even shifts quickly, the SS are swift to strike a blow with their rifle butts.

We newcomers are exhausted. The long march, the sparse food, and most of all the emotional strain, has taken its toll. The other prisoners stand for an hour in roll call, but we Jews must stand for two. Finally, we are ordered up into the attic. Twenty-seven tired and nervous men hope to get some sleep. He who sleeps nearest the stairway receives orders to always listen out for an SS guard coming up the stairs. If he hears one, he must immediately leap up, stand at attention, and report how many prisoners are present. He must also alert the other prisoners so that they will stand at attention, too. This applies both day and night.

It is cold in the attic. Several of us keep our socks on that first night to keep warm. The SS do not like that. They walk along the rows of prisoners to inspect. The poor wretch who has socks on receives a hard blow to his legs and under his heels. It is unbelievably painful. After this first punishment we can finally rest. I toss and turn on the uncomfortable mattress, and eventually fall asleep from sheer exhaustion—miserable.

SIX

"*Los! Los! Aufstehen!*" (Come on! Come on! Get up!)

This is yelled at five o'clock in the morning. How I come to hate the order "*los!*" The Germans constantly use it to move us along, to get us to work faster. I rub my eyes after the brutal awakening and run down to the basement to get in line for the toilet and sink. Have mercy on one who is not washed and dressed next to a made bed and ready to march to the dining hall when the order is given.

We Jews are not with the other prisoners in the dining hall either. They have their food and are out of the dining hall by the time we enter. Awaiting us is a cup of substitute coffee and one slice of bread each. This is the only food we will receive for the workday and we are expected to labor for many hours on this sustenance alone. We are barely able to eat this modest meal before the order is given to line up in the yard. There, prisoners are split into different *Arbeitskommandos* (work details). Some will work in the laundry, others in the carpentry shop or at nearby farms. The luckiest are those who get to work with the farmers. Now and then, they can get extra food and care. Those who work indoors, protected from the weather, are also lucky. Prison clothing is thin. It is a cold fall with much rain and sleet. We Jews must always work outdoors, most often in the stone quarry that is about 2 or 3 kilometers from the camp.

We march to the stone quarries carrying tools and equipment. On the way, the SS conduct punishment drills.

"Deep knee bends! Up, down, up, down, two steps forward, up, down! *Los*, Jewish pigs, *los*! Faster, you are going to work! This is not a vacation! Up, down!"

Some prisoners fall.

"Faster! Hurry up, you lazy rabble!"

The words slam into us while we struggle forward on the sloping terrain. If we go too slowly, the SS soldiers are quickly on us with their rifle butts. The soldiers are having fun and laugh hysterically when any of us falls in the dirt. The prisoners should not be dirty, but how can we avoid slipping and sliding on the clay-like ground? The Germans demand a clean uniform, and the Star of David must be white. We are ordered to crawl along the soaking stones.

"You are a bunch of Jewish pigs! Look at you! Get down to the brook and wash yourselves! Jewish scum!"

The SS soldiers roar at us. We are able to wash off the worst layer of dirt by crawling through the brook, but as a result we are wet through to our skin. In the cold, drizzly fall weather it is impossible to warm up again. We must work in this sodden state.

Carrying rocks is heavy work. We are split into crews of two people each. Between us, we carry rocks that weigh 20–25 kilograms on a stretcher to the camp. Fifteen or sixteen two-man crews walk slowly through the heavy wet grass with these stretchers of rocks between them. Backs bend under the weight. It feels as if one's arms are growing longer and longer. To lighten the load, I try to put a steel wire around my neck, concealed down the inside of my sleeves and around the handle of the stretcher. Under my jacket I place a couple of old socks on my shoulders so that the steel wire won't cut into my skin. It helps a little, but the heaviness remains. My hands are full of blisters that burst and ooze. The pain never heals before the next day's work.

Many are not used to manual labor, and for the older men, the heavy lifting is too much. But there is no mercy here. If a man doesn't work fast enough or takes a little breather on the hill, the SS soldiers are there immediately with their rifle butts. The blows can be many. Muscles become sore. On the road back, we proceed with heavy steps. The Germans demand that we walk with a straight back and at a steady pace. But the going is sluggish, with the rifle butts hovering over our backs. That first day shows us that the Germans view themselves as the master race.

After coming back from work, and after roll call, I get orders to wash the floor in one of the rooms. It is sparkling clean. An SS guard enters and overturns the bucket of water, right in front of me. I look confused. Why did he do that? Only a few seconds go by before he orders me to dry the floor. Laughing, he tells me to do this with a toothbrush. Rage washes over me. What kind of absurdity is this? Despair and hopelessness burst in my chest. The SS guard looks at me while he snarls "*Los*." There is nothing else to do except to start working. Why did he do that? The question is repeated continuously in my head while I sit on my knees with the toothbrush in my hand. It's not worth it to ask—here one must just obey orders. I will manage. I am angry, but what good does it do? It is good that Mamma isn't here to see this absurd situation. That night, out of pure exhaustion, I fall sleep as soon as I lay my head down.

SEVEN

Some days are easier than others, but we Jews are always picked out for the most difficult work. Luckily the road to the stone quarry goes through Falstad farm. When the SS soldiers turn away or don't feel like noticing, the farm workers slip us a few slices of bread or occasionally a glass of milk. Their sympathy warms us, and it boosts our self-respect.

The aim of this "special" treatment is to make us Jews *Untermenschen* (subhuman). The SS also want the other prisoners to look down on us. But the non-Jewish prisoners feel for us. They don't understand why we should be targeted for such tough treatment. They see the unfairness, but there's nothing they can do. There is no representative here to take complaints about poor and unfair treatment. All prisoners live under such strain. All are beaten. All are hungry and cold.

The one we call Gråbein (literally Gray Legs, or another name for a wolf) is the worst of the prison guards. He loves to use his power in the most brutal of ways. He follows Flesch's orders to the letter regarding extra torment for the Jews. Pestering the Jews brings Gråbein great pleasure. He asks his superiors to be allowed to guard our outdoor work detail. Yes, he asks to spend his free time giving us extra drills. He wishes to torture us as much as possible.

Uncle Aron has been called to the SS office. The old man knocks on the door. Inside, a loud discussion is taking place among the soldiers. Uncle thinks he hears them yell, "*Herein.*" But they didn't. When they see the old man open the door, the soldiers become hysterical. The stately and proud Uncle Aron, who practically emits rays of a good, family man, is thrown out in a rage. They yell at him. Then they hit him. They throw him in solitary confinement in the basement, which is half full of groundwater.

After three or four days, when Uncle Aron is let out, I almost don't recognize him. It is incredibly painful to see him so beaten up, to experience his bewilderment when he returns from solitary, black-and-blue from the blows he received. Swollen everywhere. The light in his eyes extinguished. Daylight is painful after so many days in the dark. I go to Uncle Aron, embrace him, and support him as much as I can. We chat together. I try to get him into the infirmary. They refuse to admit us. I lead him to Leo Eitinger,[24] a young doctor and also a Jewish

24 Leo Eitinger (1912–1996) grew up in Lomnice (today in the Czech Republic) and graduated with a degree in medicine from the Masaryk University in Brno in 1937.

prisoner. He helps Uncle as much as he can. We are able to secretly get some warm water from Odd Jacobsen[25] who works in the kitchen. The people in the infirmary feel helpless about not being allowed to treat those in need. When my finger swells up, it is infected, painful, and looks terrible. Leo manages to get a knife from the infirmary and pierces my finger while I hold a bowl underneath it to catch the pus. My finger is then washed and tied with some bandages that Johannes Rostad[26] smuggles out of the infirmary. We stand in the stairwell and hope that no Germans show up. For once we are lucky.

Fall storms arrive. The trees are naked. Falstad prison camp becomes grayer and more depressing. The prisoners have lost weight. Without hair on our heads, we all look like something the

After Germany occupied the Czech lands of Bohemia and Moravia in March 1939, he fled to Norway where he was active in bringing Czech–Jewish children to a children's home in Oslo. He worked as a psychiatrist in Bodø, but after the German occupation of Norway, his work permit was revoked, and he went underground. In March 1942, he was arrested and incarcerated until his deportation on February 24, 1943. In Auschwitz, he served as a prisoner–physician in one of the *Reviere*. After surviving a death march, he was liberated from Buchenwald in April 1945. Upon returning to Norway as one of the few surviving Jewish deportees, he resumed work in Bodø, and later Oslo. In 1966, he was appointed professor of psychiatry at the University of Oslo and he was head of the University Hospital Psychiatric Clinic. Much of his research was devoted to the traumatic impact of flight, imprisonment, and the experience of violence. A receiver of many awards, including Commander of the Order of St. Olav, he and his wife, Elisabeth "Lisl" Kohn (1914–1999), devoted their lives to fighting racism and advocating human rights.

25 Odd Wilhelm "Willy" Jacobsen (1914–2006) worked as a baker in a large Trondheim bakery. He was active in the resistance and was a member of the small Norwegian Communist Party (NKP) and was arrested on October 9, 1941, after a denunciation. He was interrogated and beaten. On December 11, 1941, he was incarcerated without trial in Falstad where he worked in logging, eventually switching to kitchen duty. In 1944, he was transferred to the German concentration camp Grini near Oslo, from where he was liberated.

26 Johannes Rostad (1885–1976) ran a bakery in Orkanger. He was a member of the city council and of the Norwegian Stortinget (parliament), representing the NKP from 1922 until 1944. A leading communist organizer, he was arrested on November 14, 1941, and spent the rest of the occupation years in Vollan prison, Falstad internment camp, and from 1944 until 1945 in Grini concentration camp.

dog has dragged in. Wounds fester, joints become tender, the hunger claws at our intestines. Everyone thinks about their loved ones, including me. How are they? What is Mamma doing? Has she made it to Sweden? Should I try to escape, cross the border? But I don't know what the situation is with Mamma so I'm unable to leave. What would these evil people do to punish her if I fled? In my mind I imagine the worst.

When I lie down each night before I go to sleep, I plan to flee. But to succeed I need contact with someone outside the camp. None of us have been allowed to have visitors in the seven weeks we have spent in Falstad, weeks that already feel like months. How will I contact someone who can help me escape?

EIGHT

The work in the quarry is difficult even for the strongest among us. None of us are used to such heavy manual labor. The older men are exhausted and suffer more than us youth. But for all of us, our arms and legs ache. An older man says that it feels like his body is decomposing. Sundays are a day off and a welcome relief. We get time to tend our ills and rest our sore muscles before a new work week sets in.

But Gråbein, our sadistic guard, does not think a day off work is beneficial. He therefore requests permission to implement an extra drill for the Jews, or else the days are so boring and without excitement. Jews should be humiliated.

Gråbein screams, "*Alle Juden auf den Appellplatz!*" (All Jews out to the yard!)

Soon, twenty-seven men are gathered in the inner yard, hidden from view by the surrounding barracks, filled with foreboding. The yard is covered with gravel. It is 70–80 meters long and 20 meters wide. Only one large, lonely tree grows here. The branches stand naked after the storms of the last few days.

"Do you see those leaves that lie in the yard? It looks untidy. Pick them up!"

I look around for a rake. But I am mistaken.

"You will crawl. Down on all fours and get to work! Not with your hands. Pick up the leaves with your mouths!"

Have I understood the words correctly? Pick up the leaves with our mouths? Yes. We have understood correctly. While we crawl on all fours, every leaf must be picked up with our lips and carried across the yard. I feel like a dog, and I can't bear to look at my friends in the same situation. We all crawl like animals, young and old alike. It hurts our knees, our arms, inside our mouths—and perhaps we feel the most pain in our hearts. SS guards stand around us with raised rifle butts, ready to beat the poor soul who doesn't crawl quickly enough with leaves in his mouth. While we are struggling on all fours, an SS guard kicks the pile of leaves we have already gathered. The leaves again spread all over the yard. The guards laugh. Behind closed windows our fellow prisoners watch what is happening. They cry together with us over this insanity. But they can't do anything to help us. Any form of resistance will be severely punished, perhaps with death.

The day's torture does not end with this madness. During the evening roll call, we Jews stand in rows once again for counting. Our joints are especially painful after crawling in the yard. Roll call takes time. He who does not stand exactly in line with the others gets fifty deep knee bends, while the rest of us must stand at attention.

Cantor Josef Grabowski[27] had fled Germany in 1937. He worked in the Jewish community in Trondheim and has the most magnificent opera voice one can imagine. The Germans know how to take advantage

27 Josef Grabowski (1911–1942) grew up in Posen (Poznan) and had his first position as cantor in Gleiwitz (Gliwice). After the "*Kristallnacht*" pogrom, he was arrested and incarcerated in Buchenwald. With the help of his brother, Leopold, who lived in Copenhagen, he was released from the concentration camp and emigrated to Norway, where he became the cantor of the Trondheim synagogue. Here he married his fiancée, Liesbeth Dorothea Wolff (1920–1943), who had followed him to Norway. Josef Grabowski was arrested on October 9, 1942, and spent six weeks in the Falstad internment camp before being deported to Auschwitz on November 25, 1942. In Birkenau he was selected for forced labor at the IG Farben Buna construction site in Monowitz, where he died on March 3, 1943. A few days later, Liesbeth arrived at Birkenau and was taken directly to her death in the gas chambers.

of this and love hearing him sing in German. He is ordered to sing. In the middle of this hell, we hear his clear tenor. In some sort of perverse moment, the prisoners and prison guards have a sense of community through the music. The cantor's last notes fade and are replaced by a sort of sentimental silence, but the quiet is broken by the barking of one of the guards' German shepherds.

"*Los, los*...get on with it...you swines...!"

NINE

The cold, sleety November day begins like all other days. We Jews are ordered to go to the stone quarry. The cold seeps into our bodies and the sleet is making us wet through to the skin as we march along the muddy, miry road to the stone quarry. Many already have colds and are coughing. Aching limbs and painful wounds make some of us walk with an unsteady gait. After the night's downpour the quarry is wet and claylike.

Three old men are ordered to roll down the rocky side of the quarry. The chosen men are Kalman Glick,[28] sixty-five years old; Moritz Abrahamsen,[29] sixty-one years old; and Swedish citizen Herman Schidorsky,[30] fifty-five years old. As Sweden was a neutral country, a

28 Kalman Glick (1877–1942) lived as a merchant in Trondheim. On October 7, 1942, he was among twenty-nine Jews who were arrested in the greater Trondheim area and taken to Falstad where he was executed on November 13 without a trial, while the chief of the Trondheim German security police, Gerhard Flesch, was inspecting the camp.

29 Moritz Nevezetsky Abrahamsen (1881–1942) had immigrated to Norway from Lithuania as a young man and worked in northern Norway until settling in Trondheim in 1920, where he ran a small business. After his arrest on October 7, 1942, the labor in Falstad was extremely difficult for him. On November 13, 1942, he was exempted from work, taken to the Falstad forest with Kalman Glick and Herman Schidorsky, and pushed into an open grave. According to the postwar exhumation of the grave, Moritz Abrahamsen was buried alive.

30 Herman Schidorsky (1887–1942) was a Swedish citizen, born in Stockholm, who had settled in Trondheim where he ran a watchmaker's shop. On November 13, 1942, exhausted from the Falstad forced labor, he had been granted a day off with

Swedish citizen really should not have been subjected to imprisonment by a government ruled by occupying powers. But Schidorsky was. These three men hesitate at the top. It is a long way down, maybe 5 or 6 meters. But down they must go! The SS guards stand in readiness to push them down. Three innocent, old men roll down. We, the other stone carriers, watch paralyzed. The shock gives me a sick feeling in my stomach. My hands clench and my muscles tighten while I watch them roll slowly down over the stones. They are horribly battered. Blood runs down their dirty faces and mixes with tears of pain and degradation. They are not able to move. I go slowly over to them and help the nearest to his feet. Like the two others, he can barely stand. The three miserable men receive orders to climb onto our stretchers that are already filled with 20–25 kilograms of stone. Even with help from others, the men are barely able to make it. Then they are ordered to sit on top of the pile of stones while we carry them back to the camp.

We start to walk. Then the beaten men are ordered to yell loudly in German, *"Ich bin ein fauler Jude, ich will nicht arbeiten!"* (I am a lazy Jew, I don't want to work!)

They must yell these degrading words over and over. The guards are entertained by this. The men cry powerlessly. I feel the tears squeezing out of my own eyes. I feel hate flare up inside me, a hate against the military power. I am young, strong, and physically fit. I don't know from where I get the strength for this heavy load. But my will is strong, and I will show these military pigs that I will prevail.

Back in the camp we get them into the barracks. Leo Eitinger tries to help the feeble trio. Clandestinely, Leo tries to deaden the pain by washing the injuries with warm water that I have secured from Odd Jacobsen in the kitchen. Johannes Rostad, our helper in the hospital block, smuggles in disinfectants. He wants to help more, but dares not. I can't even bear to imagine the consequences if the SS were to discover anything. The next morning, the three battered men are unable to get out

Abrahamsen and Glick. At the end of the day, he was killed by a gunshot and buried on top of the others in an anonymous grave. His wife, Jenny, née Savosnick (1882–1943), was deported to Auschwitz on February 24, 1943, and murdered upon arrival. The couple's sons, Michael and Moritz, managed to escape to Sweden.

of bed. Their injuries are infected and it is too painful to move. The three receive "clemency" and are allowed to remain in bed. The guards then promise that in a few days they will be able to go to Levanger Hospital.

It is the evening of November 13 and time for the ambulance transport to Levanger. We are told to carry the injured men down from the attic to the gymnasium. The three are looking forward to receiving real medical help in a clean, white hospital. There is no ambulance waiting outside though, just a truck. We are sent back to the attic and hear the truck's door close. We can't see through the vents in the roof, but we hear that the vehicle does not turn to go on the road to Levanger. It drives toward the Falstad forest. We know what that means. Soon we hear the sound of shooting.

My stomach turns. What did these three men do? Nothing. Absolutely nothing. With great sorrow and heavy hearts, we try to sleep through the night. There is no mercy here if we don't have strength for the next day's work. Should our strength falter, we will meet the same fate. I don't sleep much that night. I toss and turn on the mattress in a rage. I fantasize about escape.

I whisper to my neighbor, "Is there anything we can do?"

But he is even more depressed than I am, and is almost paralyzed by the events of the day.

The days drag by with yelling and screaming and punishments for trifles. If a pair of shoes stand a little out of line during inspection, there is a punishment drill. If a hat doesn't come off a head fast enough or if one forgets to yell one's name when passing an SS soldier, punishment comes, usually in the form of beating and kicking.

One day the camp receives the questionable honor of being visited by Flesch's second-in-command, *Obersturmführer* Julius Nielson.[31] While he inspects Falstad, his car is to be washed. I am unlucky and receive orders to wash the large car. I wash and wash. The car is spotless, totally unmarred by a single fleck after I have

31 *SS-Obersturmführer* Julius Hans Christian Nielson (1889–1948) was a German Gestapo officer and commander of the German security police and the security service in Trondheim. After the war, he was sentenced to death and executed due to his involvement in several cases of torture and other war crimes.

polished it. Now the car stands buffed and shiny without a trace of dust. *Obersturmführer* Nielson walks across the yard and glances at the Star of David on my chest. He explodes in a furious rage.

"No Jew may touch my car! How dare you allow a Jew to wash my car?"

He screams in fury at the SS guard who had ordered me to wash the car. In turn, the SS guard becomes hysterical and directs his anger at the next rung of the German hierarchy. The scolding goes down the ranks. I am at the bottom. Therefore, I must be punished. I don't understand. The car is clean, glossy, and freshly polished before them. I have exerted myself in vain in order to avoid the inevitable punishment if there was even a speck of dust to be found. I had even washed the underside of the car.

The SS soldier bellows at me to light the wood-burning stove in the guard room. I can do that, I have learned how to do that, I think. I lay paper and wood in the oven and am handed a match. I send a warm thought to my teacher, Magne Håve at the Ila School, who taught me how to make a fire in the forest. It doesn't take long before the fire crackles and warmth spreads into the room.

"Look at this mess, you Jewish pig! Clean around the oven!"

In order to wash the back side of the oven, I am ordered to crawl around the oven that stands tucked into the corner. Again and again, I have to crawl on all fours around the soon glowing oven. I shriek each time my body comes into contact with the iron. The SS guards laugh. The burns are agonizing, my knees are hurting—the oven is standing on a metal plate and that is also hot. The pain and heat are making me dizzy. How long will this go on?

"Now are you warm enough, Jew? Come, I'll cool you off."

One of the soldiers grabs my head and pushes it into the bucket of dirty water over and over again. By the end, I can barely breathe.

The soldier smiles at me. "You must be cooled off by now?"

As if this abuse isn't enough, I am told to stand on a stool. I sway as I climb up. I am ordered to stretch my arms straight out in front of my body. The handle of the water bucket is hung over my hands and, in this position, I must do deep knee bends—without spilling water. Up, down, up, down, I don't know how many times.

I am completely worn out when one of the guards yells, "*Los*. Out. Get out! Kike!"

I am exhausted and have numerous burns. I feel so downhearted that tears spring from my eyes as I exit and go to the yard. The watchtower guard sees me come from the guardhouse. He wants some entertainment too. He orders me to wriggle like a snake through the mud in the camp and then to run around the tower. I must continue this until I can barely walk or even crawl. Soon enough he tires of this entertainment and yells, "Get out of here, you stupid Jew!" Depleted of all strength, exhausted and distressed, I drag myself over to the cellar door. I must take a shower. It's the only way to get the mud out of the gray prison clothing. If my uniform is dirty when we line up for roll call, I will certainly receive further punishment.

That evening I lie on my mattress and think through the day with terror. The burns are painful. Leo tries to alleviate the pain as best he can without any first aid supplies. Every limb in my body hurts. My head is pounding from the treatment I received. This is physical and psychological terror beyond imagination. How long will I be able to cope with this? Sleep will not come. I lie awake for many hours, tossing and turning on my mattress, even though I am exhausted. I think gratefully of my wonderful childhood. When Pappa was alive. Mamma and Pappa taught me how people should behave toward each other. Where are you, Mamma? I hope you escape this fate. Tears run quietly while I clench my fists in anger and frustration. At last, sleep comes, bringing with it liberating rest.

In the morning the hill is covered with frost. The cold and dankness seep into my limbs, which feel terribly painful. All prisoners are marked by their time in Falstad. It doesn't look like there is any help to be had. I speak with my comrades and fantasize about escape. But how does one get out of a prison camp without contact with the outside world? We live isolated, as if we are on an island of solitude in the middle of Norway.

Only during the few times when Cantor Grabowski sings in the yard can I forget where I am. One evening he is ordered to sing the "Wolgalied" from the operetta, *Der Zarewitsch*, by Franz Lehár.

Es steht ein Soldat am Wolgastrand,
hält Wache für sein Vaterland
in dunkler Nacht allein und fern,
es leuchtet ihm kein Mond, kein Stern.

There stands a soldier on the Volga's shore,
Holding the watch for his Fatherland
in darkest night, alone and far,
it shines not with the moon, nor the stars.

It is a pleasure to hear this. For us it is strange to see that the SS soldiers, these inhuman bullies, have tears in their eyes when they hear the cantor's song. Are they homesick? Do they remember that they are normal family men? Maybe the song awakens their conscience for a short while? Then they bellow at us again, as if to stifle their inner voices.

TEN

November 25, 1942. The day begins like all other days in the prison camp. All is gray and gloomy. Roll call as usual, but then no march out of the camp. The Jews get orders to change from prison uniforms into their own clothes. We look at each other in disbelief. Are we going to be released? Then comes the announcement: We are going on a transport. Fear grips me. What does it mean? Are we going to Germany? What will happen to me, to us all?

Confused, we are ordered up onto a truck that takes us to Vollan prison in Trondheim. It is a long day, with unrest and fear coursing through our bodies and minds. The fear doesn't leave us when we are summoned and driven to the train station early in the evening under the heavy guard of the Norwegian police. That day in Trondheim, the police arrested all Jewish women and children who were still in the city. When we come marching into the station, the women and children are there.

In the middle of the chaos over what is happening, there is joy to see our loved ones again. The men rush to their mothers, wives, and children. I see Mamma in the midst of all the women and jump toward her. I almost make it before the Norwegian police grab me and push me back. Family members are not allowed to speak to one another here.

The state police take over the prisoners as if it's a military operation. We are told to pay attention as they need to get us counted and organized. All are ordered into the train cars. The train rolls slowly out of Trondheim station. I press my head against the window, despondence taking over me.

Now aboard the train, I get the chance to speak with Mamma. We are both emotional when we sit down next to each other. She wants to hear how I am. I tell her briefly about my experiences but try to spare her the worst. Mamma explains that Idar was arrested on October 26 in Larvik, together with his fiancée, Maja, and the rest of the Sachnowitz family. It was a dreadful time, she sighs. Mamma worked as a packager in the municipal bakery. The Germans had seized all Jewish property. The Germans took our property and home on Brattørgaten. Mamma was driven out and housed with other women in an apartment on Museumsplassen.

I see how nervous she is about what is going to happen to us. I hold her hand, which feels warm and comforting. She has many new furrows on her innocent face. I try to convince the two of us that we are going to a work camp, and that I will help her. It is important that we stay together.

"But what about Idar and Maja?" Mamma asks with tears in her eyes. I answer calmly that I'm sure we will meet them in Oslo.

The train stops in Hamar. Red Cross personnel come on board with food for everyone. The sick receive treatment, clean bandages, and medicine. It feels unbelievably good to be treated like a human being again. We remain at the station for a long while. It's as if the railroad personnel don't want to let the train continue. Do they sense the danger? We arrive in Oslo late at night on November 26. From Østbanestasjonen (East railway station) we are driven directly to Bredtveit prison, where we hear that 530 Jews were sent to Germany earlier that day on a ship called the SS *Donau.*[32] Mamma and I, and all the others from Trondheim,

32 The SS *Donau* was a large, refrigerated cargo ship, built in 1929 and operated by Norddeutscher Lloyd. During World War II, it was confiscated by the German navy

came too late for the ship's departure. But Idar and his fiancée, Maja, are on board.

As usual, we seventy-two Jews from Trondheim are given "special" treatment. We are not quartered in the prison itself, but in a barrack within the perimeter of the fence—the "Jew Barrack"—together with others who didn't arrive in time for the boat's departure. Women, children, and men lie in separate sections. I hear about the lucky young men who are sent to dig ditches at Nyland shipyard, child's play compared to the stone quarry at Falstad. Here, the guards are Norwegian Nazis. Many of them are proud to strut around in their uniforms, particularly the Hansens, a father and son who are both guards and often "play" SS. However, for those of us who have come from Falstad, they are poor imitations.

The Jewish children quickly become restless and bored. Leo Eitinger realizes immediately that they need something to do and arranges lessons for them. Mamma gets even more taciturn. Her usually happy eyes are no longer smiling. For the many unemployed prisoners, it is a time of restless wandering inside the perimeter of the fence, heavy thoughts, and nervous conversations. The conversations revolve mainly around what happens to those who are sent to Germany. Some simply wish to go there too, in a naive, fearful belief that if everyone is together, we can also help each other. Colds and bronchitis wreak havoc. Melancholy sneaks in everywhere and is contagious.

The head of the state's Department of the Church, Minister Ragnar Sigvald Skancke,[33] visits Bredtveit prison one day. He meets some inmates and greets my uncle, Aron Mendelsohn, whom he knows from his time as a professor at the Norwegian Institute of Technology in Trondheim. He also taught Uncle Aron's youngest son, who is a civil

and used for transports between Germany and Norway. In January 1945 it was sabotaged by the Norwegian resistance and beached in the Oslofjord.

33 Ragnar Sigvald Skancke (1890–1948), a professor of engineering at the Norwegian Institute of Technology in Oslo. On the day of the German invasion on April 9, 1940, he was appointed minister for labor affairs in the Nazi government under Vidkun Quisling. In the Quisling cabinet, formed on February 2, 1942, after the Nazi coup d'etat, he had the influential post of education and church affairs which he used to nazify schools and persecute anti-Nazi teachers and priests.

engineer. Uncle Aron is therefore under the impression that he and the minister know each other and asks Skancke if he can help get him, his wife, and his son a Swedish passport. In fact, *Tante* Thora is Swedish born, and their son, Henrik, is married to a Swede. But Skancke the Nazi answers quickly and sharply that he has nothing to discuss with the Jew Mendelsohn. I followed the conversation from a distance and see that the answer hits Uncle Aron like a bullet. He bows slightly and turns away with tears in his kind eyes. Uncle Aron never really got over that degradation.

I have been imprisoned since October 7 and now it is Christmas. How long shall I be denied freedom? We have a break from work at Nyland, and we get an extra slice of bread and a little meat. A Christmas package from my good friend Bjørn Trønsdal brings me joy. And so, Christmas passes. New Year's Day 1943 arrives with new hope. All the prisoners agree that this year will be better. Surely it can't be much worse.

Mamma becomes sick with a high fever. She lies in bed in the barrack without any form of help. I also get a fever as a result of the brutal treatment in Falstad. Mamma sits with me for many hours while I lie in the barrack. We speak about everything that has happened and try to comfort each other.

The prison doctor Hans Eng[34] is Vidkun Quisling's personal doctor. He does not want to treat Jews. But Sigrid Helliesen Lund[35] the

34 Hans Eng (1907–1995) was a Norwegian collaborator, SS volunteer, and chief physician of the Nazi Nasjonal Samling organization. He was also the chief physician of the Bredtveit prison and supervised several executions. The resistance movement unsuccessfully attempted to assassinate him more than once. After the liberation he received a rather mild prison sentence. Eng remained a Nazi throughout his life.

35 Sigrid Emilie Helliesen Lund (1892–1987) was a Norwegian pacifist and women's rights activist, cofounder of the Norwegian section of the Women's International League for Peace and Freedom and the refugee help organization, Nansenhjelpen. In 1939 she obtained asylum in Norway for a number of Jewish children from Nazi-occupied Prague, and in 1942 she engaged in helping persecuted Norwegian Jews. In 1944, she fled to Sweden where she continued working for the refugees. After the war, she became active in Quaker aid and reconciliation activities both in Norway and abroad.

lovely woman from the National Health Office, urges him to examine me. He ascertains that I am sick and have a high fever, and sends me to Bots prison[36] where I am placed in a medical cell. During the weeks in January and February when I am lying in the medical cell, five prisoners escape from Bredtveit including my two cousins, Josef and Leif Klein,[37] and Arnold Levy and his sons. One way or another they had contacted people outside the prison. During a fifteen-minute break for fresh air, they climbed over the two-and-a-half-meter high fence. They cut through the barbed wire on top of the fence and lowered themselves onto the other side. They ran to a waiting truck, and were gone.

In the meantime, Leo has also been a patient recuperating in the same gray cell as I. He suffers from back pain. The cell has a small window. The small amount of daylight brings sunlight into our cell, which lifts our spirits, and we remember that there is light in the world outside these walls. Dr. Gordon Johnson,[38] that noble man, treats us both. He gives me the diagnosis of rheumatism and arthritis. The only ointment he has to treat me with is chloroform, which is placed on cotton bandages around my limbs. This should take away the pain.

After a while, Dr. Johnson warns us that we will probably be picked up by the Norwegian state police. But when the state police arrive, Johnson refuses to hand us over. He claims that Leo and I are too sick. But the state police chief, Jonas Lie,[39] demands that we come. He

36 Botsfengselet was the old main prison of Oslo, inaugurated in 1851.

37 Josef Klein (1904–1970) was the son of Henoch Klein (1876–1946) and Anna Ruth, née Paltiel, who died in 1914; the mother of Leibe Leif Klein (1921–1989) was Henoch's second wife, Rose. The Klein family ran textile shops in Trondheim and were actively engaged in the city's Jewish life. During the first Norwegian purge against Jewish business they lost the family's main store. When their house was confiscated, parts of the family hid with a non-Jewish family in the mountains. As some members of the Klein family prepared to cross into Sweden (they successfully skied for over 32 kilometers through deep snow), Josef and Leif were arrested and interned in Falstad. After a few weeks, they were taken to the Bredtveit prison in Oslo from where they were able to escape and eventually make it to Sweden.

38 Gordon Johnson (1905–1983), an Oslo physician and a fervent Lutheran, specialized in the treatment of mental patients. In 1957 he founded the Modum Bad Psychiatric Sanatorium for mentally ill patients.

39 Jonas Lie (1899–1945), a Norwegian Nazi politician, served as minister of police

threatens that if we are not released, all civil employees in Bots prison will be arrested and transferred to Grini.[40] Gordon Johnson offers to help us run away. He knows people in the resistance who have avenues of escape. Leo and I discuss the offer, but dare not accept his help. What would the Germans do to Mamma and Leo's foster mother, Nora Lustig, who are both prisoners in Bredtveit?

Toward the end of February, Leo and I are seized by the state police and brought back to Bredtveit. A strange atmosphere of foreboding prevails there, a contagious nerve-consuming unrest. Some of the prisoners are gone—they have received Swedish citizenship. Some are Swedish born and some Swedes who had become Norwegians through marriage received their Swedish passports back. Those who are married to Swedes manage to arrange Swedish passports through family members who were able to escape. In principle, the Germans cannot touch those with Swedish passports. But in a few cases the papers don't arrive in time or the Germans rip them to pieces. Even after Minister Skancke's harsh words, Uncle Aron, Aunt Thora, and Henrik wait in hope for passports but they never arrive.

and was a close aide of German Reichskommissar Josef Terboven. Lie was a key figure in the persecution of the Jews in Norway.

40 *Polizeihäftlingslager* Grini was the largest German internment camp in Norway. An unfinished prison for female delinquents in Bærum near Oslo, it was turned into a camp for Gestapo prisoners in June 1941, in which 20,000 Norwegian, Polish, French, Soviet, and other prisoners were incarcerated. The camp was extremely crowded with the number of prisoners reaching 5,400 by 1944. Of the 768 Grini prisoners who did not live to see liberation, most died after deportation to Germany. Conditions did not deteriorate to the level of the German concentration camps under the Inspektorat der Konzentrationslager (Inspectorate of the Concentration Camps, IKL), but many inmates feared violence from the guards. After the liberation, collaborators were interned in the camp and its name was changed to Ilebu prison.

PART TWO

IN THE KINGDOM OF THE DEAD

ONE

There are now 158 Jews in Bredtveit prison. In addition to us from Falstad and Trondheim, the Germans have arrested more Jews since the departure of the SS *Donau*. On February 24, 1943, we are driven to the wharf in Oslo. The steamer SS *Gotenland* is moored there. The large vessel looms before us. The trucks stop near the ladder leading up to the deck. I have no doubt that we are going on the same journey as the others before us—to Germany.

We are quickly chased off the back of the trucks and are told to line up on the wharf. Then we receive our orders: "On board!" The wind and snowflakes hit us from the fjord. The mist from the frost forms small, white clouds. No one knows if the tears that fill our eyes come from the wind or from our hearts. But there are tears.

Painful scenes play out as women and men are separated from one another and are sent down into separate cargo holds on the boat. Married men say farewell to their wives and children. Children hang around the necks of their parents and want to stay with them both. The

View of the SS *Gotenland.* United States Holocaust Memorial Museum, courtesy of Oskar Mendelsohn.

elderly are slow to board. The Germans hit them hard. Many cry out for help. But there is only brutal separation here. The eldest aboard the ship is eighty years old, the youngest only one and a half.

The departure from Oslo is sad. We are not permitted to stand on the deck and see the land retreat behind us. But I imagine how the landscape disappears, a long stretch of land with noble, proud mountains. Adieu, my precious homeland.

In the cargo hold, we men sit tightly packed against each other. It's as if the darkness of night has laid itself over the day, a heavy foreboding of what is to come. *SS-Untersturmführer* Klaus Grossmann[41]

41 *SS-Untersturmführer* Klaus Grossmann (1912–1945). From 1941, he worked for the Gestapo office of Jewish, Masonic, and Church affairs. He commanded the SS guards aboard the SS *Donau* and SS *Gotenland* on the transports that took the Norwegian Jews to Auschwitz. From mid-1943 he led the office of the German security police in Drammen and was in charge of regional German counterterrorism, an organization that was meant to discredit the resistance movement. Due to a failed operation, he was demoted and took his own life shortly before liberation.

is the commander of the guards aboard the ship. He is used to such transports. Three months earlier he transported 530 deported Norwegian Jews on the SS *Donau*. He speaks to us, tries to calm us, and assures us that those who are fit for work are going to Germany to work. Families will be allowed to live together. We choose to believe him although I am doubtful as I heard Grossmann remark to a young woman who was singing together with her children that they should go on singing while they are still alive.

The food we receive is sparse. There is little water. Cleanliness has been relegated to the lowest priority. After a while, the air in the cargo hold quickly becomes heavy. We have only a few buckets into which to relieve ourselves. During these dark days I am full of fear: What will happen to Mamma and myself? Is there any way for me to help Mamma? I still feel sick. Will we meet Idar where we are going? He was so sick himself, and he has been in Germany for three long months already. Where are we going? I also think about Pappa, with whom I had such a close relationship. Idar and I had to grow up far too quickly. Mamma was never happy again after his death. And now this.

The SS *Gotenland* sails through the Øresund, the strait between Denmark and Sweden. Through the small windows in the side of the vessel I can see the distant lights of the Swedish cities. When will we be allowed to go into a city and see the lights again? Some become seasick. Heavy odors rise up from frightened men. Their faces are gray and grimy from fear and tears.

On February 27, after three days of traveling, the SS *Gotenland* glides slowly toward the harbor. We have reached our destination. We are quickly chased onto the deck. Where are we? The mist from the frost hangs over the water and there is snow on the ground. Waiting on the pier are hundreds of soldiers, dressed in green, lined up ready to receive us. They are armed. Some of the soldiers have barking German shepherd dogs on leashes. The city glimmers in the distance. We understand that the boat has docked in Germany. The city is called Stettin. We can see the train station and train tracks next to the dock. Boxcars stand ready.

"*Los, los, schneller!* Disembark!"

Many fall as they are pushed down the ladder. I see that Mamma is about to collapse from the pressure behind her. But I am not allowed to go over and help her. I hold my breath: Will she make it down safely? It goes well. I am freezing, shivering.

On the pier there is a roll call. Then we are herded into the boxcars. The soldiers yell. The dogs bark. We are packed so tightly in the empty cars that it is impossible to sit down. The train rolls out, at first in fits and starts, then rhythmically. We sway in rhythm with the track as the train car leans into the bends. After half a day the train comes to a halt. We have reached Berlin.

TWO

We are driven to the synagogue on Levetzowstrasse, one of the few synagogues that the Nazis have not yet destroyed. It is being used as a collection point to gather Jews for transportation. There is a throng of people. Following police raids in Berlin over the last few days, close to 2,000 Jews have been arrested.

All newly arrived prisoners get a form thrust into their hands. We are told to sign a declaration that all our property and assets in Norway will be transferred to the German state, which, in return, will provide for us for as long as we live. What is this supposed to mean? Mamma and I discuss it, but we have no choice. We sign the form.

I begin a conversation with some Germans who are about my age. With Mamma's help I understand that they want to know where we come from. They are Jews, studying agriculture in a bid to go and work in Mandatory Palestine. Their parents thought that this would be their salvation, that they would be able to leave Nazi Germany and go to Mandatory Palestine. But the British didn't grant them entry permits. All thirty people in their group were arrested.

The atmosphere in the synagogue is electric. So many worried people. So much fear. I can barely breathe. My heart hammers uncontrollably. Sweat drips off me. I walk toward the exit to get a little fresh air. There I see a large group of uniformed, armed soldiers guarding us. I get a glimpse of the street scene: countless flags with swastikas and numerous groups of Hitler Youth, singing and marching. The scene fills me with fear.

We have a terrible night, locked in with so many people crowded around us. I am sweating terribly. I want to move so badly, walk back and forth a little, get some fresh air, but I'm soon ordered to sit. I slip down into place next to Mamma. We hold hands, but need not speak. Each knows what the other is thinking.

We fall asleep, but not deeply. We awake suddenly. A formidable Allied bombing sets in over Berlin. The bombs fall just next to the synagogue. Windows shatter. The electricity cuts out. The building shakes. Fear takes hold. Many cry. Children scream hysterically. The SS soldiers are terrified, panic grips them. They are running around with pistols in their hands and yelling that whoever moves will be shot. Slowly and carefully I place my arms around Mamma. I see the despair in her eyes. I try to calm her down. Many have shards of glass stuck in their bodies and are bleeding. But no one receives help. Through the empty windows we see flames from nearby fires. They draw unpleasant light formations against the black sky. More bombs explode over the city. Anti-aircraft artillery shoot with their deafening roar. After a while, all is still.

No one sleeps more that night. When the first rays of daylight filter in through the broken windows, silence lies ghostlike over the synagogue. But it is not long before the message comes that we are to be taken to the train station. More than 2,000 people, adults and children, must gather their personal belongings and quickly leave the synagogue. Families try to stay together. There is much screaming and yelling for children, who would rather play than crowd themselves into the waiting trucks, despite the night's frightening experience. In the damaged building, total confusion prevails. We are told to stand in the trucks and we are driven away, passing by bombed-out homes. Some places are still burning. No one tells us where we are going.

The train station in Berlin is huge. Hundreds of SS soldiers, with death's-heads on their uniform collars, and Hitler Youth stand ready next to the cattle cars as we march in. I am trembling just from the screaming as we are herded onto the platform. We are freezing, hungry, thirsty, and scared. Carrying our backpacks or small suitcases, we move as quickly as we can. The yelling of the SS soldiers drowns out all other sounds, "*Los, los*, get on with it…"

I almost can't believe what I am seeing. SS soldiers are kicking and whipping people into the cattle cars. Young boys, younger than me, are herding us with whips and sticks yelling, "*Los, schneller, schneller, los, verdammte Judenschweine!*" (Hurry up, faster, damn Jewish pigs!)

The blows fall arbitrarily, indifferent to whether they strike adults or children. We eventually fall over each other as we are whipped forward at an unimaginable pace. The Nazis bellow in a German I can barely understand, words I never learned in school. My German friends from the synagogue translate for me. They are in the same group as we are.

I am behind Mamma in the line. She struggles to get into a cattle car. One Hitler Youth hits her with his stick. I yell. Guns point at me for a moment. The experience at Falstad and advice from the Jewish youth remind me to hold my tongue. I can't do anything to help Mamma. In the wagon I can finally place my arm around her shoulder. One car is designed to hold six horses and two men. We are sixty or seventy frightened Jews packed together. We can barely move. Half a loaf of bread for each is thrown in. A jerry can of water is being divided. There is one bucket in which to relieve ourselves. The cattle car door is then closed and locked from the outside. We are caught in a trap.

Over 2,000 ill-fortuned, frightened people are being transported toward the unknown. Healthy, sick, young, and old alike. A child's cry pierces the stillness. The wail breaks the dismal silence that fell when the doors were locked. It's as if the child's tears give us all permission to let out our despair. The train starts rolling.

THREE

The monotonous sound of the train wheels—da-dum, da-dum, da-dum—stops. It is the night of March 3, 1943. A second of deafening quiet before the door is unbolted from the outside and opened. We are chilled to the bone after almost three days in the locked cattle cars—we are so cold that we barely feel the fresh and icy cold air that streams in.

"*Raus, raus!*" (Out, out!)

The screeching hits us with force. We have been standing so tightly together that we have barely been able to move. Our legs are numb after standing still for so long. It takes a little time before we manage to move ourselves.

"Los, los! Out with you, Jewish pigs! *Los, los!"*

In the fog of the morning light I catch a glimpse of low buildings as far as the eye can see. I see double rows of barbed wire. Soldiers on guard aim their weapons directly at us. I hold Mamma's hand tightly. Hundreds of frightened prisoners exit the long train. Shock is visible on their faces.

"*Los, los!* Out, forward march! Leave your bags! They will be brought to you!"

The German orders crackle in the air. Prisoners pile out of the cattle cars. Many of them fall. I lift Mamma down to the platform that is slippery with snow. I turn to help others, but am stopped by a rifle butt.

"*Los! Aufstellen! Schneller, schneller! Kommt heraus!*" (Orderly! Faster! Out!)

Now the orders come from the loudspeaker.

"Forward. Move. Men to the right, women and children to the left."

Their commands crash down upon us. Large German shepherd dogs on tight leashes lunge at us. The noise level rises to a violent cacophony that fills our heads and drowns out every thought. We are surrounded by SS soldiers and prisoners in striped uniforms. Contrary to what we have been told, the prisoners don't look happy to be working. They are skinny, bent, and ashen. They walk quickly everywhere. The prisoners retrieve our luggage.

One of the bowed men whispers to me, telling me to remember that here I am healthy, no matter what. He warns me to be careful, that many of the guards are insane murderers. Then he disappears as quickly as he showed up.

Men to the right, women to the left? We were promised that we would be allowed to stay together. Reluctantly Mamma and I release our grip on each other's hands. We are brutally moved along, each in our own line. Our bewilderment is complete. Women yell for their men.

Men call to the women and children, "We will be together." But no one hears us. No one answers.

A mother loses her grip on her child's hand and the child heads toward the father. But the SS know no compassion. The child must follow the mother. Another mother allows herself to be fooled when an SS guard lifts her child in the air and gives the child a hug. Then he sets the child down and shoots the child right in front of the mother. She sinks to the ground only to be driven back in line. I can hear her screams long after she is taken away.

The daylight reveals the dismal atmosphere in all its horror. We are lined up. Women and children separately, crying, pale, and afraid. Men in their own area, just as fearful. Women and children are chased onto a truck. Luckily, they are spared from standing here for hours, I think. They will certainly be taken to their new quarters. As Mamma climbs up onto the back of the truck, she turns for a short moment. Our eyes meet. Mamma stretches her arms toward me. Then, the truck drives away.

An icy wind sweeps over the platform. The horrible noise—SS soldiers roaring commands, German shepherds barking, the reverberation from the loudspeakers—hinders any form of conversation. The Norwegian prisoners stand in a row alongside hundreds of other prisoners. *Hauptsturmführer* Aumeier[42] walks along the row and asks how old we are. I answer that I am eighteen years old. He points to where I should stand. The prisoners who are over forty years old are immediately ordered to march and are herded across the platform by SS soldiers with weapons at the ready. Where are they being taken?

42 Hans Aumeier (1906–1948), *Sturmbannführer* from 1944 onward. As an early member of the SS, he was personally known to *SS-Reichsführer* Heinrich Himmler. He advanced through several Nazi concentration camps, always displaying extremely violent behavior toward the prisoners. In 1942 he was appointed *Schutzhaftlagerführer* (leader) of the inner administration of the Auschwitz I *Stammlager* (main camp), but one year later he was sent to the newly established Vaivara concentration camp in Estonia as punishment for corruption and theft. Here his crimes and atrocities continued. After a short period in a subcamp of Dachau, Aumeier was made commandant of the Grini camp in January 1945. After the liberation, he was handed over to the Polish authorities. He was tried and executed as a war criminal.

In single file we move slowly past a smartly dressed SS officer on the platform. A discreet pointing with his thumb shows who goes to the right and who goes to the left. Those who look strong go to the right. I am in the right column. We wait anxiously for several hours. What we are waiting for we do not know. We get no food. We are thirsty. Snow falls softly. Elegantly dressed officers walk around, chatting, watching us. I feel their stares and try to make myself invisible.

Only twenty-seven male Norwegian Jews from the SS *Gotenland* transport survive that first selection. We are moved to a neighboring camp, Buna-Monowitz or Auschwitz III,[43] which lies 6 kilometers from Auschwitz itself. Here there aren't as many barracks as in the main camp or Birkenau. For the time being there are only around 2,000 prisoners here. We are taken to Barrack 9, which has space for 250 people. We Norwegians try to keep together in a corner. The young Germans from Berlin get berths just next to ours. Being with people we know gives us some sort of feeling of togetherness.

Tired, scared, and weary, we collapse on our bunks that are so close together there are barely passageways between them. A straw mattress, a straw pillow, and a woolen blanket lie on each bunk. Three bunks high. There are two chimneys in each barrack, connected with

43 The concentration camp Auschwitz III was established in October 1942 in Monowitz (today, Monowice), some 6 kilometers from the Auschwitz I main camp. Monowitz prisoners performed forced labor at the neighboring IG Farben Buna site, constructing a huge factory for synthetic rubber. Most of the Norwegian Jews who were selected for forced labor upon arrival in Auschwitz were sent to Monowitz. By New Year of 1943 the camp held 4,000 inmates. By February 1943, only 2,000 were still alive. The high loss of life was caused by the grueling forced labor that the prisoners had to perform in freezing conditions without adequate clothing or food, and alongside the extreme violence perpetrated by the SS guards and prisoner functionaries. Most Norwegian Jews succumbed to the horrendous living and working conditions. When a *Revier* was installed, IG Farben insisted that only 5 percent of the prisoners could be ill at any one time, so prisoners who were too weak to work were sent to Birkenau for gassing and replaced with new arrivals. Some 11,000 people lost their lives this way, while 1,670 prisoners were killed at the building site or in the camp infirmary. On January 18, 1945, the Monowitz camp was evacuated and most prisoners were sent on a death march. When the Red Army liberated Monowitz, only the weakest prisoners were found in the camp.

an air duct to warm up the large room. But it is barely warm in the poorly insulated barracks. The wind blows right through the wooden walls. We can peep out through the gaps in the planks in some places. A bucket for a toilet, for use during the night, is placed in the front part of the barrack.

I cannot fall asleep that first night in my bunk. Where is Mamma? Will I meet Idar? These questions and the foreign sounds around me make me restless. Finally, I get a little warmer under the woolen blanket and fall asleep. But I wake up all too often. The next morning, I feel as though I have not slept at all. I wonder if the others are just as tired.

"*Los! Aufstehen! Antreten!*" (Get up! Get in line!)

The sound of this roaring reverberates in the barrack at five o'clock on this icy cold, March morning. We put on our clothes at full speed and are chased into the frozen yard outside the barrack. Drifting snow lashes at us. The darkness of night rises around us. I can see prisoners in striped pajama-like uniforms standing and shouting orders to their fellow prisoners. This is the first time I experience this. The one in command is called a Kapo or work foreman. Most who are selected to be Kapos are German criminals whom the SS have taken from their prison cells. They had been imprisoned with life sentences, convicted for one or several murders. A green triangle together with a prisoner number is sewn onto their prison uniforms. Green triangles mean criminals; murderers, thieves. These are men who have already demonstrated their brutality.

All prisoners have triangles sewn onto their prison uniforms. In this way, the SS can quickly see to which group a prisoner belongs. We get a gold Star of David and a red triangle with an "N" for Norway. Political prisoners have a red triangle. Gypsies and so-called asocials have black triangles. Jehovah's Witnesses and *Rassenschänder* (non-Jews who are married to Jews) bear violet triangles.

Some Kapos view their job as an honor and it appears that they take pleasure in creating fear. In their own eyes they are better than the other prisoners. But the SS guards punish the Kapos whenever they feel like it; they obviously don't think the Kapos are better than the others. The camp administration also appoints Jewish Kapos. The SS know what it is doing—pitting brother against brother.

That first morning in the camp, we get a cup of substitute coffee and a piece of bread. The coffee is cold and the piece of bread is hard, but it is something to put into our stomachs. We eat outside the barrack. I am far from full. We are quickly hustled back into the barrack so we won't be able to communicate with others. A young boy around my age whispers to me that I should watch out for the Kapos, because they can kill me, too. I look at him disbelievingly. He nods, barely, trying to make me understand that he is telling the truth.

Anxiously, we sit together at one end of the barrack and discuss what will happen now. Other newly arrived prisoners also sit in groups and speak in their native tongues, surely about the unknown that awaits them.

"Attention!"

In comes a group of SS officers of various rank. The leader begins to speak in a friendly tone saying that if we just do as the SS say, everything will be alright and our imprisonment will be a breeze. With that, the friendliness is over. The officers demand that we surrender our clothes. We protest loudly. One of the officers demands that we hand over our good Norwegian sweaters and mittens. We do not want to give them these garments. We try to refuse. The officers laugh at us, and ask if we really believe that we will be allowed to keep these clothes. I hide behind some large men and hope that the officers don't see my hand-knitted sweater. But soon I am standing in just my shirt.

All 250 men in the barrack are commanded to shower. It will be nice to have a shower, I think naively. All our clothes lie in a heap on the floor. Shoes are required to be tied together in pairs. All we own is taken away. We stand stark naked in line.

Then we are chased out of the barrack. With our hands covering our private parts we run in fierce cold over the hard, frozen snow. The cold burns the soles of our feet. It is about 50 meters to the next barrack. To my great surprise, standing there is a group of six barbers. They have scissors and shaving knives at the ready. They call us one at a time, in alphabetical order. As Paltiel is my last name, I stand in line for a long time and see how hair is almost torn off the prisoners. The barbers' equipment is blunt, and it requires strength and pressure to use it. Hair is removed from the entire body—the head, armpits, chest, groin. It hurts like open sores. We look strange, like newly sheared sheep. Fortunately, there are no mirrors. But we see each other.

We are sent on to the washing barrack. We are frozen through, our teeth chatter, and we rub our bodies to keep warm. It is well below freezing. We stand in a large room with showerheads above us, but no faucet with which to regulate the temperature or pressure. The water shifts between ice cold and burning hot. First, I'm frozen, then the water is burning me. The soap is a disinfectant that stings and burns our already painful skin. Many suffer, but there is no help. I look down over my inflamed body and long for my clothes.

Now we are herded further toward the clothing warehouse. We are handed thin prison uniforms and funny flat hats with stripes. I receive a hat that is totally the wrong size, but am able to trade it for one that fits. We receive wooden clogs to wear on our bare feet. The orders are clear. Both our uniforms and hats must always be clean. Each time we meet a uniformed soldier or officer we must take off our hat to show subservience to the master race. Our bodies shiver from the cold. I had contracted rheumatism in Falstad and now my limbs are aching. I hope Mamma doesn't have to go through the same process. What is happening to her?

Our next stop is the physician. Professor Berthold Epstein,[44] who arrived on the first prisoner transport from Oslo on November 26, 1942, checks us. I tell him my medical history. But he has gained valuable experience over the course of the past three months and

44 Berthold Epstein (1890–1962) was a Jewish professor of pediatrics, and director of the children's clinic at the German Hospital in Prague. In March 1940, he fled to Norway and became head of the pediatric clinic of the Oslo University Hospital. Forced to resign after the German occupation, he instead concentrated on tuberculosis research. On October 27, 1942, he was arrested and on November 26, he was deported aboard the SS *Donau*. In Auschwitz-Birkenau, he was selected to assist notorious SS doctor Josef Mengele (1911–1979) as a prisoner-physician in research on noma, a deadly malnutrition-induced disfigurement of the facial tissue. In spite of efforts to bring about his release, Epstein was a medical forced laborer until the liberation of Auschwitz. He served as a witness in Soviet war crimes trials and eventually settled in Prague, where he became head of the Bulovka Hospital children's clinic.

whispers carefully to me, "There is nothing wrong with you." Luckily, I take the hint.

Once more we are commanded to line up. We are going to be tattooed. The *Blockälteste* (the barrack chief), gives us a piece of advice on the way. He tells us that we will get a number tattooed on our left arm. We are told to forget our names because here we don't have a name, just a number. Here you are fit for work or you are dead. I stare at my arm. It burns with pain. The tattooing needle stabs me again and again. Now I am marked, demoted from being Julius Paltiel to being *Häftling* (prisoner) number 105362. No, damn it, they will not be allowed to break me! I am Julius Paltiel I will live! I am only eighteen years old.

Tears are not far away. We continue, and we are handed a spoon and a bowl. All we own in this world is a spoon and a bowl! Take pity on the one who doesn't manage to keep tabs on his belongings—he doesn't have much of a chance. It is difficult to get hold of a new spoon and bowl, and without a bowl, one cannot receive one's ration of "soup." We grind the handles of the spoons against rocks so that we can use them as knives. In this way we can split the daily bread ration into several small meals.

FOUR

In the barrack the *Blockälteste* swings the whip. He is the boss in here and he in turn answers to the SS. If the SS is not pleased when they inspect the barrack, it is he who suffers. Here the pecking order operates by the book. If the barrack chief or Kapo gets punished, that punishment is then passed on to all of us. The Jews are on the lowest rung of the hierarchy. The punishments we are exposed to can consist of anything from a thrashing to being hanged, or a collective punishment that lasts for many hours. Push-ups, jumping jacks, jogging around the barrack for hours. If an SS soldier wishes to torture a prisoner, he can whip him in the yard for hours, until the prisoner dies, either of exhaustion or from the beating he has received.

The *Blockälteste* lectures us about how we should make our bunks. In German, it is called *Bettenbau*, and it is a very exact procedure. The thin straw mattress must be shaken and flattened evenly, the straw pillow likewise. The woolen blanket must lie flat. Sheets do not exist. The process must follow these precise steps. The bunks are packed tightly. Cheating is not tolerated here. The *Blockälteste* checks how the bunks look every day. If he is not pleased, everything is ripped off, accompanied by cascades of screamed insults and abuse. The SS come frequently to check the cleanliness of the barracks. Are there dust balls on the floor? Are the bunks uniformly made according to regulation? One would think that the Germans wanted to win the war by making beds properly! *Sauberkeit ist Gesundheit* (Cleanliness is health) is written on one of the rafters.

March 1943. For the first time we meet some of the 530 Jews who were transported from Norway on November 26 the previous year. Only ten are still alive. They look ghastly. Skinny, pale, malnourished, and deathly tired. My brother, Idar, is not among them. I ask about him. I am told that he is up the chimney. When I don't understand, they explain that he was gassed.

Slowly, the horror dawns on me. They tell me that Idar wounded his leg so he went to the infirmary. That day, all who sought assistance at the infirmary were sent directly to the gas chamber, without question or a medical examination. I actually don't understand the meaning of this word "gassed." I have never heard of it. Gassed to death? But I do understand that Idar is dead.

I think about Mamma. Hesitantly, I ask if anyone knows where the others from our transport are. I want to see Mamma so badly. The others look at me with tired, dull eyes and whisper, "Gassed." My whisper is like an echo. Now it dawns on me that Mamma is also gone, dead. I ask desperately about Uncle Aron, Aunt Thora, and the others. The answer comes tonelessly, "Gassed." This horrible word makes my head ache, makes it burst. Gassed, gassed, gassed, screams a voice inside of me. I close my eyes, cover my ears, but the word still hammers over and over again. Gassed, gassed, gassed!

I feel lonely, isolated, totally left alone. I am in a vacuum. Only Henrik Mendelsohn is still alive. All the others are gone, dead, gassed to death. I want to be alone. I remove myself from the others and allow my tears to flow freely. I almost wish I was dead.

We are inexperienced prisoners. We still don't know what a concentration camp really is. We haven't yet understood how much we must keep our guard up. Our fellow prisoners' warnings about the brutality of the SS soldiers did not help the Caplan brothers[45] from Tromsø. We were told that one of them was joking around. The *Blockälteste* saw him. Punishment came immediately. He let loose on the Tromsø boy with his rubber baton. The older brother rushed to his brother's aid. Immediately, an SS guard came to the *Blockälteste*'s rescue. Two full-grown, powerful men hammered away at the young Norwegian boys. After a short while they lay dead before the prisoners. I couldn't believe that such brutality existed, even after my experiences at Falstad. It is completely surreal, beyond all imagination. Fear seeps deep into my being. I feel total loneliness and horror.

45 On June 18, 1941, the Gestapo arrested a large number of young male Jews in northern Norway and took them to the new *Polizeihäftlingslager* Südspitze in Tromsø. From there, the prisoners were transferred to other camps and eventually to Grini. Four of the sons of the Tromsø merchant Daniel Caplan (1870–1943) and Anna Sara, née Glück (1870–1930) were taken there and deported on the SS *Monte Rosa* on November 26, 1942. Another son, Pincus Caplan (1910–1993), avoided arrest, but the other four brothers—Jacob (1903–1943), Solly (1908–1942), Hertze (1913–1943), and Chonne "Conrad" (1922–1945)—were sent to Auschwitz for forced labor. Their sister, Cecilie Levin (1910–?) was married and lived in Denmark from where she managed to flee to Sweden on October 3, 1943. After two weeks in Monowitz, Solly was beaten to death by an SS man while Hertze died of starvation on March 3, 1943. Jacob was killed two weeks later, on March 19. Conrad was selected for the Birkenau *Sonderkommando* and worked in the *Kanada* warehouses, where the belongings of arriving Jews were sorted in order to be reused. In January 1945, he was sent on a death march toward Buchenwald and ended up in the Dora-Mittelbau concentration camp in the Harz mountains, where he died shortly before U.S. forces liberated the camp on April 11, 1945. Daniel Caplan was dispossessed and arrested on October 26, 1942, and released due to old age. He was rearrested on November 25, 1942. In February 1943, he was deported with 157 Norwegian Jews on the SS *Gotenland.* When the group reached Auschwitz-Birkenau on March 3, 1943, Daniel Caplan was taken directly to the gas chambers.

FIVE

The land is all flat. Marshy and damp. Not a tree to be seen. Just a simple church rises against the horizon. The impression of an eternally gray landscape forces itself upon us. The whole world is gray and heavy, a yoke upon our shoulders. An oddly sweetish vapor oozes into our nostrils. We have already become used to it. The smell comes from the crematorium and forces its way in everywhere. It's in our nostrils, in our clothes—we cannot get rid of it. The smell of burning human flesh. It attacks us like a nightmare, with unbelievable power. It is a constant reminder of what awaits us.

The crematorium ovens burn day and night. The smoke rises like a scream toward heaven, a shifting black monument. Each time the gas chambers have been used, they must be emptied of corpses and aired out. But after a few minutes, the next group sentenced to death is led in. The *Sonderkommando* has the loathsome task of pulling out the dead. Sometimes a prisoner finds someone from his own family among the corpses.

Jews from all over Europe are gathered here. All occupations are represented. Scientists and doctors are put to work with the most degrading tasks, such as writing out false death certificates. Dentists are assigned to pull the gold teeth from the mouths of gassed prisoners. Craftsmen are commanded to use their training to build factories for the Nazi war machine.

We live each day in a paradoxical situation. For example, the Germans belong to a civilized nation and are taught to enjoy good music. Many SS officers love music. They can be moved to tears when they hear a talented violinist, even if the musician is a Jew or a Gypsy. The prisoner might even fall into favor and get extra food rations. But women and children are treated as roughly as men. Here one only lives if one is able to work. If not, the road will lead directly to the gas chambers and crematorium. This is Auschwitz.

In Buna-Monowitz we are forced laborers for IG Farben. The industrial giant "rents" us from the SS, and the SS is paid for our labor. We must work for the military power. In the factory, methanol, chemical gasoline, and imitation rubber are manufactured. The area of the camp is huge, some 50 square kilometers. We are comparatively few prisoners, at least for the time being. But each day new transports of Jews arrive from all over Europe. They are put to work building new barracks. Soon 20,000 prisoners live here. We all speak different languages, but we learn German by rote. First, we master the words that are being used by the SS all the time, words that are not found in a regular dictionary. My Norwegian companions and I are quickly spread out among the thousands of other prisoners. I no longer have anyone with whom to speak Norwegian, no one who is close to me. Here one can only depend on oneself.

The first order for my work detail is to tear down the church that stands alone in the middle of the field outside the camp area. We are escorted to work by a small army of SS soldiers armed with rifles and batons. I think the SS are scared that we will escape. But where could we possibly hide? There is not a single building, not even a bush to hide behind.

The day starts with roll call at five o'clock in the morning. Work begins at six o'clock. Every single morning, we are painstakingly counted before marching out from the camp barracks to work. The counting upon our return is just as meticulous. The camp orchestra plays marching music when we leave and when we return to make us walk faster. The orchestra consists mostly of professional and talented musicians. Many of them are from the Hilversum Radio Orchestra. I soon notice Herman Sachnowitz[46] from Larvik among the orchestra musicians. He plays the trumpet. Herman is the brother of Maja, my brother's fiancée. The orchestra's director is Stanisław Bronek,[47] a

46 Herman Sachnowitz (1921–1978), the son of Larvik shopkeeper, Israel Leib Sachnowitz (1880–1942), was a musician. He survived Auschwitz III–Monowitz by playing the trumpet in the Buna camp orchestra. His father, his brother Elias (born 1911), and sisters Rebekka Rita (born 1915), Marie (born 1919), and Frieda (born 1923) all perished in Auschwitz, while his brother Frank (born 1925) was taken to the Natzweiler-Struthof concentration camp and killed so that his skeleton could be incorporated in the anatomical collection of the Reichsuniversität Strassburg.

47 Stanisław Bronek established the Buna camp orchestra with over twenty musicians in early 1943. He was succeeded by the military musician Bernard Dondalsky, followed by trumpet player Bronisław Stasiak.

tall, thin man from Poland who leads the orchestra with a firm hand. Eventually, the orchestra develops such a high professional standard that it's often used by the SS for concerts and entertainment.

Some days, fog lies low and dense over the swampy region so we must stand for hours in the roll-call square. The SS soldiers dare not let us out to work. In the foggy weather there is always a chance of escape. But where would a miserable wretch from the camp hide? If a prisoner was lucky enough to make contact with or reach a Pole, he would hardly receive any help from him. They would send him back, and the punishment would be hanging. Only when the fog lifts are we sent to work. It is icy cold. Snow and dampness force their way through our bodies. The thin prison uniforms offer little protection. I have no gloves and the pockets in my clothes are sewn shut. Many get frostbite on their hands and feet, but the "superior race" don't care about a little frostbite. I get dizzy from standing at attention for hours. I sway a little. A cold sweat breaks out over my body. If I fall, I risk punishment. I manage to stay on my feet.

The first period of work stretches until noon. Large buckets with watery soup, which we call "Buna-soup," are driven out to the worksite. Some 1,200–2,000 men stand in line to get their single scoop of the strange gray-green liquid, which gives us no notable nourishment. When I eventually get my bowl of soup, it is seldom warm. But it is a lovely break from the strenuous work that is always under heavy guard. Now I can sit down on the hill, relax for a brief moment, chat with my workmates, or close my eyes for a short while. But even during these few minutes of rest, the guards don't leave us in peace. They do whatever they can to hound us. Every movement is being watched. If any motion is too sudden, the nervous guards are on us at once with flying fists. And they know where it hurts the most.

After an additional five or six hours of hard work, we march back to the camp. We are frozen through, exhausted, hungry, and thirsty. Many can't bear the thought of one more day of this forced labor and fall out of rank. They are quickly killed. Some drop from exhaustion. We try to pull them up out of the mud, drag them with us. Then it's roll call again, and the eternal counting. I become used to the sight of dead friends and no longer have the strength to grieve for them.

Julius Paltiel's mother, Kaja Ruth Paltiel (1895–1943). Photo Collection, Yad Vashem Archives (YVA), 15000/14233785.

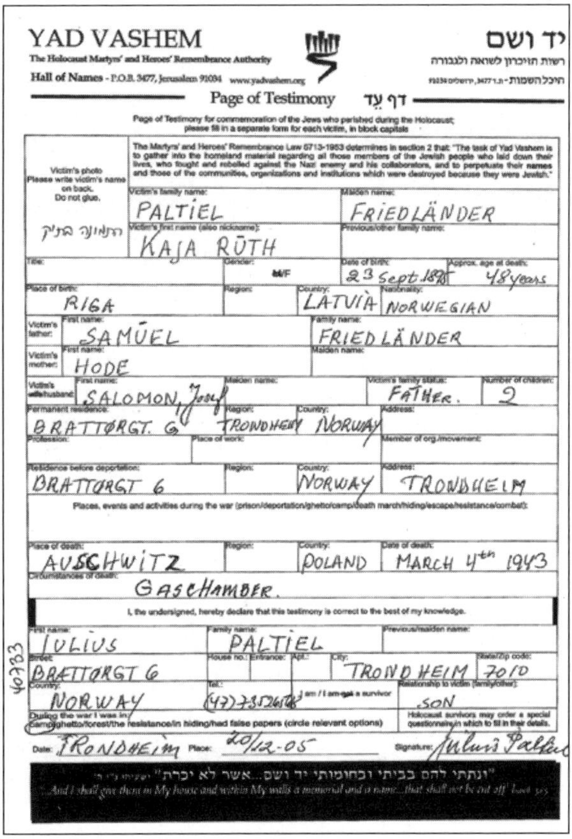

YAD VASHEM
The Holocaust Martyrs' and Heroes' Remembrance Authority
Hall of Names - P.O.B. 3477, Jerusalem 91034 www.yadvashem.org

יד ושם
רשות הזיכרון לשואה ולגבורה
היכל השמות

Page of Testimony דף עֵד

Page of Testimony for commemoration of the Jews who perished during the Holocaust; please fill in a separate form for each victim, in block capitals

The Martyrs' and Heroes' Remembrance Law 5713-1953 determines in section 2 that: "The task of Yad Vashem is to gather into the homeland material regarding all those members of the Jewish people who laid down their lives, who fought and rebelled against the Nazi enemy and his collaborators, and to perpetuate their names and those of the communities, organizations and institutions which were destroyed because they were Jewish."

Victim's photo. Please write victim's name on back. Do not glue.

Victim's family name: PALTIEL
Maiden name: FRIEDLÄNDER
Victim's first name (also nickname): KAJA RŪTH
Previous/other family name:
Title:
Gender: M/F
Date of birth: 23 Sept 1895
Approx. age at death: 48 years
Place of birth: RIGA
Region:
Country: LATVIA
Nationality: NORWEGIAN
Victim's father: First name: SAMŪEL Family name: FRIEDLÄNDER
Victim's mother: First name: HODE Maiden name:
Victim's husband: First name: SALOMON, Josef Maiden name:
Victim's family status: FATHER.
Number of children: 2
Permanent residence: BRATTØRGT. 6
Region: TRONDHEIM
Country: NORWAY
Address:
Profession:
Place of work:
Member of org./movement:
Residence before deportation: BRATTØRGT 6
Region:
Country: NORWAY
Address: TRONDHEIM
Places, events and activities during the war (prison/deportation/ghetto/camp/death march/hiding/escape/resistance/combat):
Place of death: AUSCHWITZ
Region:
Country: POLAND
Date of death: MARCH 4th 1943
Circumstances of death: GASCHAMBER.

I, the undersigned, hereby declare that this testimony is correct to the best of my knowledge.

First name: JULIUS
Family name: PALTIEL
Previous/maiden name:
Street: BRATTØRGT 6
House no.: Entrance: Apt.:
City: TRONDHEIM
State/Zip code: 7010
Country: NORWAY
Tel.: (47) 7352618
I am / I am not a survivor
Relationship to victim (family/other): SON
During the war I was in: camp/ghetto/forest/the resistance/in hiding/had false papers (circle relevant options)
Holocaust survivors may order a special questionnaire in which to fill in their details.
Date: TRONDHEIM Place: 20/12-05 Signature: Julius Paltiel

40733

"ונתתי להם בביתי ובחומותי יד ושם...אשר לא יכרת" ישעיהו נ"ו ה
"And I shall give them in My house and within My walls a memorial and a name...that shall not be cut off" Isaiah 56:5

Kaja Ruth Paltiel, Page of Testimony, Yad Vashem, The Central Database of Shoah Victims' Names, Hall of Names, item no. 5867334.

Julius Paltiel's brother, Idar Paltiel (1919–1943). Photo Collection, YVA, 15000/14233786.

Idar Paltiel,
Page of Testimony,
Yad Vashem, item no. 5867335.

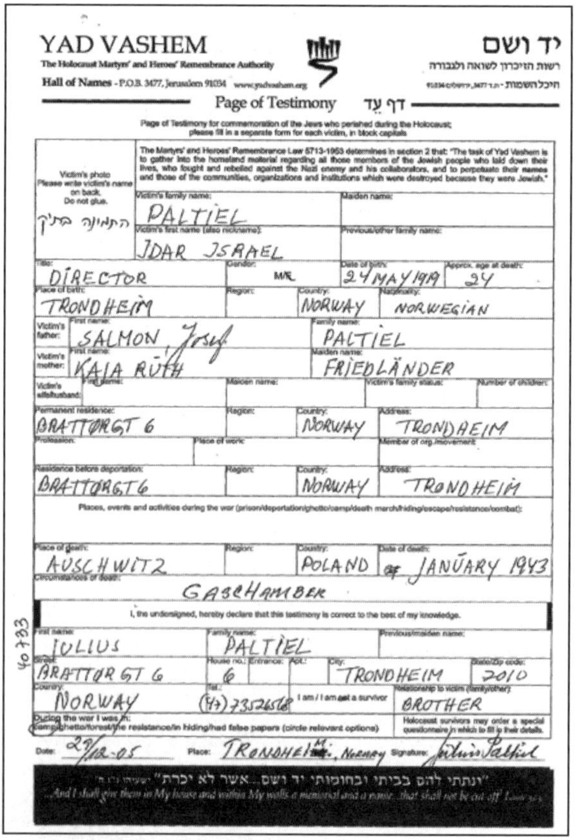

YAD VASHEM
The Holocaust Martyrs' and Heroes' Remembrance Authority
Hall of Names - P.O.B. 3477, Jerusalem 91034 www.yadvashem.org

יד ושם
רשות הזיכרון לשואה ולגבורה
היכל השמות

Page of Testimony דף עֵד

Page of Testimony for commemoration of the Jews who perished during the Holocaust; please fill in a separate form for each victim, in block capitals

The Martyrs' and Heroes' Remembrance Law 5713-1953 determines in section 2 that: "The task of Yad Vashem is to gather into the homeland material regarding all those members of the Jewish people who laid down their lives, who fought and rebelled against the Nazi enemy and his collaborators, and to perpetuate their names and those of the communities, organizations and institutions which were destroyed because they were Jewish."

Victim's photo. Please write victim's name on back. Do not glue.

Victim's family name: PALTIEL
Maiden name:
Victim's first name (also nickname): JDAR JSRAEL
Previous/other family name:
Title: DIRECTOR
Gender: M/F
Date of birth: 24 MAY 1919
Approx. age at death: 24
Place of birth: TRONDHEIM
Region:
Country: NORWAY
Nationality: NORWEGIAN
Victim's father: First name: SALMON Josef
Family name: PALTIEL
Victim's mother: First name: KAJA RUTH
Maiden name: FRIEDLÄNDER
Victim's wife/husband: First name:
Maiden name:
Victim's family status:
Number of children:
Permanent residence: BRATTØRGT 6
Region:
Country: NORWAY
Address: TRONDHEIM
Profession:
Place of work:
Member of org./movement:
Residence before deportation: BRATTØRGT 6
Region:
Country: NORWAY
Address: TRONDHEIM
Places, events and activities during the war (prison/deportation/ghetto/camp/death march/hiding/escape/resistance/combat):
Place of death: AUSCHWITZ
Region:
Country: POLAND
Date of death: JANUARY 1943
Circumstances of death: GASCHAMBER

I, the undersigned, hereby declare that this testimony is correct to the best of my knowledge.

40733

First name: JULIUS
Family name: PALTIEL
Previous/maiden name:
Street: BRATTØR GT 6
House no.: 6
Entrance:
Apt.:
City: TRONDHEIM
State/Zip code: 7010
Country: NORWAY
Tel.: (47) 73526518
I am / I am not a survivor
Relationship to victim (family/other): BROTHER
During the war I was in: camp/ghetto/forest/the resistance/in hiding/had false papers (circle relevant options)
Holocaust survivors may order a special questionnaire in which to fill in their details.
Date: 29/12-05
Place: TRONDHEIM, Norway
Signature: Julius Paltiel

"ונתתי להם בביתי ובחומותי יד ושם...אשר לא יכרת"
"...And I shall give them in My house and within My walls a memorial and a name...that shall not be cut off"

In the evenings we are often ordered outside again to build roads between the barracks. New barracks are being constructed every day. Therefore, many more roads must be built to connect the barracks. The roads within the camp must be straight as an arrow. To begin with, these roads which are made of earth erode in the damp, rainy climate. But after a while they become so solidly packed that it's as if they are made of asphalt. When I finally lie down in my bunk late at night, I am totally worn out after fourteen to sixteen hours of hard manual labor. If we even pause while working, the guards yell and accuse us of sabotage.

The SS soldiers and Kapos cannot speak normally. They only know how to bellow. The soldiers roar fiercely at us all the time using the worst expressions imaginable. We prisoners try to whisper encouraging words to each other. If the guards see that we are making contact with one another, they yell immediately, "*Halt Maul!*" (Shut up!) We are not allowed to speak to each other while we are working but fortunately, we can help each other after the work day is over. We sit on our bunks and chat, often about the cruelties of the day.

During "lunch" one day, I am sitting with my soup bowl and to my horror, I see one of the green-clad tormentors coming in my direction. I quickly look away; if the SS soldier thinks that I am looking at him, it can provoke a severe beating. Is it me he has spotted? I look up cautiously and find that the soldier has stopped in front of another boy. I breathe normally again—I have been redeemed at the last second. The SS soldier takes the boy's hat and flings it into the field where we are not allowed to go.

"*Die Mütze holen, Judenschwein! Schnell!*" (Hurry up! Get your hat, Jewish pig! Quick!)

The boy looks at him. He knows that if he goes to get the hat, he will be killed for trying to escape. If he doesn't get it, he will be punished for not obeying orders. The boy prefers to be beaten. After twenty-five blows from the soldier's baton, his legs are barely able to carry him back to the camp. One month later the boy is no longer alive.

SIX

New prisoner transports arrive continually. New people with hopes and dreams that are crushed the moment they set foot on Auschwitz's soil. The number of *Arbeitskommandos* grows. One work detail is put to work fencing in the factory area of about 50 square kilometers.

I am assigned to work in the third work detail. It consists of 1,800 men. We must empty cement bags from train cars. Each sack weighs over 50 kilograms. We have to carry them on our backs, out of the train cars to the warehouses. We hurry back and forth. The guards, clothed in warm woolen coats over their uniforms and with cigarettes dangling from the corners of their mouths, watch our every move. In thin prison uniforms we toil like animals, while our stomachs scream for food.

"*Los! Los!* Get a move on! Run!"

It is unbearably heavy to jog with cement sacks on our backs when the rain has turned the solid ground to a sea of mud. The weight bears down on us. Our arms and backs, and maybe our necks most of all, become stiff from all the lifting to which we are unaccustomed. We jog the entire day with cement sacks on our backs. There is a never-ending amount of sacks. One of the prisoners loses his grip on the paper sack and it falls to the ground and bursts. There seems to be no end to the beating and abuse the prisoner receives. The SS soldiers call it sabotage, and use the opportunity to cripple him for life before our eyes. The warning is clear: Here is what will happen if you try to sabotage the work.

For this forced labor, the employer IG Farben pays the SS four German Marks per day for each and every prisoner. If one of us is sick, he can stay in the infirmary at the expense of IG Farben for a maximum of eight days. If the prisoner is not restored to health after this period, the road leads to the gas chamber and the chimneys of the crematorium oven.

Due to the damp climate and the insufficient food, we get sick easily. Several prisoners often collapse in the middle of work. But no matter if one collapses from sickness or exhaustion, he must wait until the end of the day to go to the *Revier*. The *Revier* is a barrack like all the others, and just as poorly managed. Here too, prisoners must often lie two to a bunk because of a lack of space. During the course of the first night, many die. Those who suffer from dysentery and diarrhea are placed in a special block, while those with tuberculosis or other types of injuries and suffering are placed wherever there's space. Infection is rampant.

Among the thousands of prisoners are many trained physicians including professors of most medical and surgical specialties. Those who are permitted to work in the *Revier* use their knowledge to do their best to help the sick even if medicine and other necessary remedies are scarce. The nurses are all men and come from a range of occupations. Many of them do an extraordinary job with the little they have at their disposal, while others appear harsh and inhuman.

I get *Grippe* (the flu). I feel the fever coming; my body shakes from the cold. My teeth chatter. While standing in line to go to the doctor, my legs are trembling. I have a long work day behind me. The doctor examines me scrupulously. Am I really bad enough to get a bed? Luckily my fever is high enough. I am allowed to lie down. My body relaxes even though I have a stranger lying next to me in the bed. The space is so small that when one turns, the other has to turn too. All the berths are occupied by two patients. In the nearest bunk to me is a boy with tuberculosis. Another has sores over his entire body. The food is just as poor and sparse as elsewhere in the camp. Many of the sick are crying from festering wounds and pain. Here one is lucky just to be allowed to lie down. I lie in bed for three or four days before I am again thrown out to work, despite the fever still in my body. This is death's entryway.

It is the Jewish holiday of Pesach (Passover). This type of holiday is not celebrated here. But some of the more religious boys remind me that it is the first Seder—the evening of the first day of Pesach. I sit together with Herman Sachnowitz from Larvik. We speak about our different family traditions for this special evening. We share memories.

I myself dream of the large dinner table at the home of Aunt Thora and Uncle Aron. Over twenty family members are guests. My aunt and uncle have always hosted the whole family on this holiday evening. I see before me the white damask tablecloth, the white porcelain, the silver candlesticks with lit wax candles. The smell of soup, of fish. The small talk surrounding me in the barrack seemingly becomes the conversation around the festive table. I hear Uncle's beautiful voice while he reads the blessing over the wine, and the children's traditional question, "*Ma nishtana halaila hazeh mikol halailot?*" (Why is this night different from all other nights?) I taste the unleavened bread and the salted egg. All are symbols of the Jews' Exodus from Egypt. Upon their hasty departure, the bread didn't have time to rise, and the salt water is to remind us of the Jews' tears. Here in the camp there is a lot of salt water.

The days blend together, imprinted with empty grayness. Life is drudgery, with constant kicking, beating, and punishment. But the SS soldiers generally know not to hit so hard that we are unable to work. It does not serve the SS if we lie in the infirmary or die too soon. They need our labor.

Roll call often takes several hours. Thousands of men must line up and be counted. The count from the morning roll call must match the count in the evening, factoring in the sick, those who have died during the day, and the newcomers. Although we stand five in each row and 100 in each group, it appears that the unit responsible for counting us still has trouble. They yell, "Attention" and "At ease" between their counts. They don't care that we are freezing, hungry, and deadly tired. Many collapse from exhaustion during these hours and more than a few die.

Twenty thousand exhausted prisoners march in from work to the strains of the prisoner orchestra. An SS officer bellows something to us. I am exhausted and inert and I am not alone in these feelings. Therefore, many of us don't hear what the officer is yelling. But eventually I understand the message: Two men will be hanged today. They did not obey orders. I am paralyzed by fear even though such executions have become everyday occurrences. One day one prisoner is hanged, another day four pay with their lives in this way. I don't want to watch. I just stare emptily into space. I can't do anything to help anyway. The SS soldiers are an armed, superior force that makes any type of help impossible. And what does it matter if I cry? I have no tears left. I live in a senseless world. It is almost unreal. So unbelievably evil! How can a people like the Germans support such ideals, a people who used to be a cultured nation? But as a prisoner, I think mostly about tangible matters: food, water, sleep, and how to avoid the gas chamber.

I am not restored to full health after my visit to the infirmary. I am still in bad shape. I can't even bear the thought of carrying bags of cement. With the help of my friends, I manage to join a different work detail. Now I must roll pipes made from cement. This is not an easy job either, but we have five men to roll them into place. Then I am transferred to yet another work detail. Here the work consists of raising steel beams with a hand winch. Here, too, several people work together. In this way it is possible to rest a little between turns on the winch. The most important thing is to give the impression that one is working hard all the time—this is our protection.

During our lunch break, I lay eyes on some British military prisoners. They are also put to work. What does the Gestapo care? I drift toward the British men and get as close as I dare without being noticed. I call to them cautiously in my school-level English, and ask how the war is going. One of the men replies that the Germans are retreating. I smile and go back to my place. But I hadn't noticed that one of the stalking SS guards, whom we call the "Buna-lion," had seen me speaking with the British prisoners. He immediately reports to the *Kommandostelle* (command post) that prisoner number 105362 spoke with a British man. Soon I am called for interrogation.

I am scared. I have no idea what the SS will do to me. I stand at attention and report that *Häftling* 105362 has arrived. The SS officer comes right up close to me. He is elegantly dressed in a tight, green uniform with his regimental cap placed smartly on his head. In his hand is a little whip. He is wearing beautiful leather gloves. He kicks my wooden clogs with the tips of his elegant shoes. The officer towers over me. He opens his mouth, which is level with my eyes, and shrieks something that I don't understand. I stare into the hole of his mouth with fascination, his uvula hopping up and down in time with his words. He asks me whether I, a Jew, have spoken with the British men. I reply that I haven't. He lets his whip slide playfully around my face. Then he hits.

"Are you telling the truth, you pig?"

In halting German, I reply that I am telling the truth and explain that I cannot speak English, nor can I understand it. I am Norwegian. The SS officer bobs back and forth and looks over my head. Then he gives the order that the punishment will be twenty-five blows with a baton. If he hadn't believed me, I would have been sent to the gallows. I am commanded to lie face down on a bench. A large, powerful SS soldier takes a rubber club in his hand. He starts hitting me. The club meets my lower back and bottom hard and with precision. The soldier tells me to count the blows.

"*Eins, zwei, drei…*" (One, two, three…)

My voice is strong at the start, but becomes weaker with each blow that meets my back.

"*…dreizehn, vierzehn, fünfzehn…*" (…thirteen, fourteen, fifteen…)

It is terribly painful, and the soldier has not yet finished.

"*…vierundzwanzig, fünfundzwanzig.*" (…twenty-four, twenty-five.)

I am barely able to mumble. I breathe heavily, but I bite back my tears. I slowly lower my legs to the ground and rise. My body is in complete pain. It takes many days before I am able to sit again.

The work becomes heavier and heavier. At the same time, we become skinnier and more exhausted with each passing day. As if the torment isn't enough during the day, *Wanzeen* (bugs) plague us at night. Bedbugs creep out of the walls when the lights go out in the barracks in the evening. They invade the bunks, wander over my body, latch on, drink blood, and wander on. It's a never-ending stream of crawling insects, lice and fleas included. We itch and burn in our sleep, so much so that our bodies don't get the rest they so badly need. It doesn't help either that we are smoothly shaven over our entire bodies. We often have lice checks. If lice are discovered, the prisoner is first beaten black-and-blue and then disinfected. The strong chemical wash inflames the skin and burns terribly. The most favorable conditions for lice are the seams in clothes, where they can multiply quickly. The warning "*Eine Laus—dein Tod*" (One louse—your death) is carved into the beams in the barrack. But the insects cannot be avoided, even if I often wash both myself and my clothes. We only have cold water to help us in this matter, though. We get clean clothes once every second week. Cleanliness is a problem, but I try to make the best of the situation. It helps my self-respect. I rub my gums with a finger, so that I won't also get scurvy.

At night we sleep from sheer exhaustion. For those who are suffering from dysentery, the nightly bucket is used frequently. There are only two buckets for 250 men. Next to them sits a prisoner who is the night watch. His pay is an extra ration of soup. The night watch's responsibility is to make sure that the bucket doesn't overflow. When it is full, the next user is sent out to empty it in the latrine, which lies a short distance from the barrack. He who is unlucky enough to have to empty the bucket has ruined his night's sleep.

I quickly learn to hear how high the level of urine is in the bucket. I don't want to go out into the cold. I hold it in. Usually, going to the latrine is a welcome break as it's like a social gathering. Here we sit in a row, often with *Scheisserei* (diarrhea), and the latrine becomes a rumor exchange. There is always someone who knows something. Here we learn about the course of the war. Who has been gassed lately. Who is sick and who we can help. Here we trade a crust of bread for a cigarette that someone has managed to acquire. In spite of its smell and unpleasantness, the latrine is a refuge.

The worst job a prisoner can be ordered to do is to empty the latrine. We must bail the contents of the latrine into large wagons and then empty them outside the camp. The smell pursues us for days. Even if I am able to wash myself after doing this work, the stench lingers in my nostrils. This duty is often used as punishment. The Kapo sends a newly arrived prisoner to empty the latrine. He passes out from the smell. The Kapo laughs and uses his stick on him. The prisoner refuses; he can't do the job. The SS are called in. The punishment is brutal and revolting. Alongside the roar of laughter from the SS guards, the prisoner is thrown into the latrine. Each time he struggles out from the thickly flowing mass, the soldiers beat him down again. In the end, the prisoner dies from overexertion. The SS soldiers have achieved their goal.

SEVEN

The double barbed-wire fence is complete. It is electrified. If a prisoner touches the fence, he will be caught in death's grip. Now the Kapos take over guard duties. We can no longer run away. The barbed wire blocks our way. The German Kapos are even more inventive than the SS. They gladly grab the first and best thing they find to beat us with—an iron rod, a steel bucket. Many prisoners are seriously injured. I, as well as the others, develop hypersensitivity, like animals. It is no longer enough to see with your eyes, to hear with your ears—you must use all your senses. You must learn to feel when someone is watching, and to respond appropriately. Even if I am standing still, it must appear as if I am working. Your position and body language must signal activity. The Kapos have been taught well by the SS—they even use the same language as the SS. We hear them constantly yelling, "You lazy Jewish dog! Damned assholes! Get moving! *Los, los!*"

If one Kapo thinks I'm not working hard enough or if he's not pleased with the way I do a job, he may report me to the SS. Many are sent to the Bunker (the punishment cell). There is no hell like it. The cell's floor space is less than 60 square centimeters and still it is not unusual for three or four men to be crammed in. You cannot sit or lie down. Each one must stand. For several days. The cell door is only a little over 50 centimeters high, so prisoners must crawl in. The toilet is a bucket. The air stands still in the dark cell. More than one prisoner goes insane.

A fellow prisoner talks back to an SS soldier. We others listen and admire his style. At the same time, we are fearful about what his punishment will be—maybe even death. Today the SS guard is in a good mood, though. Now we will "play" a little, he thinks. But it can wait until the work day is finished, so that the punishment strikes the entire work detail. It is better for the SS if fellow prisoners get angry with the prisoner who provoked the communal punishment. At six o'clock we are back in the camp and have been counted and registered. Five men in a row, 100 men in each group, twenty groups, 2,000 men.

The SS soldier announces that now it's time for a little fun. "Deep knee bends. Up, down, up, down, faster, three steps forward, up, down. Lie down on the ground. Push-ups. Up, down, up, down. Jump—three hops forward. *Nah, los, los*, go faster!"

Many fall. Some prisoners are so exhausted that they cry. I am also unimaginably tired. Up-down, up-down, jump, three steps forward! The hours pass, we jump around like marionettes. Some prisoners can't take it any longer. They run into the electric fence. I look toward the fence, the last way out. My knees are in pain, my body will no longer obey me, dizziness carries me away. I am a robot. Up-down, up-down. Finally, the punishment is over. We are ordered to return to the barrack. There we can sink into the fleeting forgetfulness of sleep, at least for a few hours anyway.

It is always cold here, summer and winter alike. I am always freezing. Dampness lies like a blanket over Auschwitz. Many of my Norwegian friends are no longer alive. A few were transferred, but mostly within the camp, so I don't see them often. I know that Leo Eitinger is working in the office of the *Revier*, writing false death certificates. Others have also obtained indoor work in the kitchen or laundry. Herman Sachnowitz plays in the camp orchestra. Sammy Steinmann[48] works as a medical orderly.

I work outdoors. It is summer but I don't know sun or warmth, even when the sun beats down from a cloudless sky. Someone mentions that today is July Fourth, Independence Day in the U.S. But there is something else that is familiar about this day. I remember: It is my nineteenth birthday. One year ago, I celebrated my birthday in Norway.

48 Samuel Leon "Sammy" Steinmann (1923–2015) was the longest living Norwegian Holocaust survivor. On September 21, 1942, he was evicted with his family from their home in Aker near Oslo. One month later, he was arrested by the Norwegian state police, incarcerated in Bredtveit prison, and subjected to torture by Norwegian Nazis. In November 1942, he was deported aboard the SS *Donau* with his brother Harry (1920–1943) and another 530 Norwegian Jews. On arrival in Birkenau, Harry was murdered, whereas Sammy was tattooed with the prisoner number 79231 and sent to Monowitz where he worked as a window cleaner and later as an aide in the infirmary. While a high percentage of prisoners lost their lives on the January 1945 death march to Buchenwald, Harry survived.

It never crossed my mind that the year ahead of me would be so long and so painful. There's not much light in the future either. Will the coming year give me my freedom back at last?

My limbs are extremely painful. Rheumatism has taken hold. One day, someone asks for an electrician. I bluff. I want to be indoors. I succeed. My new fellow workers quickly see through my lie, but they help me. I can't even read an electrician's drawing. I don't know anything more about electrical connections than the average person. But it works for a while.

Death is my companion. Fellow prisoners die around me. Sometimes, when depression washes over me, I think about death as an escape. But I have decided: I will survive. I will bear witness.

I am at work as usual on a cold winter's day in the beginning of 1944. I am moving plasterboards the size of a wall with three other prisoners. The boards are terribly heavy and we have to carry them up several flights of stairs. The stairwells are narrow. We are exhausted. I am sweating and freezing simultaneously. Beads of sweat are running down my face. I feel that a fever is taking hold of my body. I feel pain all over. I dare not yield, even if all I want to do is to lie down in a clean, white bed. But that is just a fantasy. I know very well where I am. The bed I dream of does not exist here. I drag myself up the stairs.

My joints begin to swell and stiffen. I faint. My friends carry me over to a bench. I get to my feet again. But the weight of the next plasterboard is too much. My legs betray me again. I'm on the ground. I have fainted again. When I regain consciousness, one guard allows me to sit hidden on the floor until we march back to the camp. He's risking punishment, and possibly his life, for this act of humanity. I ask myself, "Is this the end? Is the gas chamber my next and final stop?" I dream about my room back home in Trondheim with its view over the roofs of Brattørgaten; I see my mother before me serving the most incredible soup. Then I come to my senses. I don't want to die. I am only nineteen years old.

We must march together back to the camp but my legs won't carry me. My friends drag me along. Without their help I would never have made it back. During the evening roll call my friends hold me upright. At last, I am back in the barrack and retrieve my soup bowl. I need whatever nutrition there is from the watery soup.

I drag myself over to the doctor's office. The line is endless. I am alternately asleep and awake. Several hours pass before my number is called. From far away I hear 105362. The doctor takes my temperature and pulse. I have a fever of 42.3 degrees Celsius. My pulse is 120. My blood sedimentation is 87. He listens to my chest. The diagnosis is double pneumonia with rheumatic fever. I am more dead than alive. Nonetheless, I must go through the shower in the washing barrack with the others. The cold water runs over my gaunt body while I hold tightly to the wall so as not to fall. I am sent naked out into the dark and intense cold. My body shakes, my teeth chatter. Finally, I get to the hospital barrack. Then I get lucky. An old acquaintance, a Polish Jew, is the head of the barrack and finds me a lower bunk where I can lie alone. I wouldn't have had the strength to climb up onto a higher bunk.

God, to be able to lie down is so good. I almost faint from exhaustion. It is past midnight. With half-closed eyes I see the nurse shake his head. He seems to be saying that there's not much life in me. Some wet and cold sheets are being wrapped around my chest but I barely register this. Then I sink into the darkness of unconsciousness. In the middle of the darkness I sense a strong white light, a drawing force. But I fight against it and choose life.

My blanket is being pulled off me. Slowly I awaken. A doctor, Professor Waitz[49] from Strasbourg, is bending over me. He grips my

49 Dr. Robert Elie Waitz (1900–1978) was a professor at the University of Strasbourg and leader of the French resistance in the Auvergne region. In July 1943, he was arrested by the Gestapo in Clermont-Ferrand and imprisoned at the Drancy internment camp. From there he was taken to Auschwitz. On October 10, 1943, he arrived in Auschwitz where he was selected for forced labor at the IG Farben Buna factory along with 250 Jewish prisoners. At Monowitz, he became a prisoner-physician and leader of the in-house clinic of the *Revier* where he established a laboratory and did his utmost to help fellow prisoners. After the January 1945 death march to Gleiwitz and subsequent train ride, he served as a prisoner-physician on the Buchenwald typhus ward. After the liberation, he helped the Americans organize healthcare for the liberated prisoners. He was reappointed professor at the University of Strasbourg in 1946, and he became the president of the Amicale

wrists and elbows with the attentive hands of a physician and listens to my chest. He confirms the earlier diagnosis. He should know as he is one of Europe's best-known lung specialists. He informs me that he doesn't have any medicine but tells me to take it easy and that he will get me some sodium salicylic acid pills to relieve some of the pain and fever.

Every two hours pills are thrust into my mouth. I swallow them with substitute coffee. I have to try and eat the daily soup ration, but I almost vomit from the pain and fever. But I force in spoon after spoon of the watery soup, and soften my bit of bread by dipping it in the soup as well. No matter how little nutrition this gives me, I need it.

After a couple of days my fever falls to 40.8 degrees Celsius under my arm. A little progress, anyway. While the thermometer is under my arm, the nurse takes my pulse. I stretch my arm toward him. It hurts. I twist and the thermometer falls to the floor and breaks. The nurse is furious. The broken thermometer makes him see red. He drags me out of the bunk and punches me on the ear. I collapse to the floor and crawl back into my bunk, dizzy with pain.

Here, nurses don't wash the sick like in hospitals back home. Here, each of us have to manage on our own. Swollen joints cause intense pain. I am not capable of leaving my bed. My legs won't carry me. I can't even walk over to the sink. As a result, I get scabies, and lice and bugs are crawling over my sick body more intensely than ever before. Small pests spread infection from one patient to another. Red spots and distended joints—I can't even look at myself. The itching and burning is maddening. I am in such poor shape that I constantly nod off. In my sleep I scratch myself until I bleed. I am a pitiful sight.

The hospital ward is overcrowded. Two patients per bunk. I have been lucky so far in that I have had a bunk to myself. But one night a seventeen-year-old boy from the Netherlands is placed in my bunk. He is extremely sick. He speaks dazedly about a long trip with a boat to America. He believes that he is standing at a railing, urinating over the edge into the ocean. But it is on me and my blanket that he urinates. I

des Déportés d'Auschwitz et des camps de Haute Silésie (Association of Deportees from Auschwitz and Camps in Upper Silesia). He was a witness in several war crimes and crimes against humanity trials against Nazi perpetrators.

can't do anything about it, though. Early in the morning, in his final cramps of death, the boy turns around and excretes on my face. Now I will get a clean mattress and blanket.

In the bunk above me, another youth from the Netherlands is deathly ill from tuberculosis. He is so weak that he doesn't eat the little ration of soup he gets, but gives it to me instead. I eat it without allowing a single drop to spill, in spite of the danger of infection. I want to live.

As I begin to recover—and no longer fall asleep all the time—I start to pay attention to my fellow patients. At the moment of death, some of them moan, some rattle. Most of those around me die. As soon as a nurse notices that a person has died, he makes sure that the corpse is taken away. When the nurse returns again, he is already bringing in a new patient.

From my lower bunk, I am astounded by the thin legs I see slowly pass by on their way to the "bucket." I forget that I must certainly be just as unpleasantly skinny myself. My thirst is intolerable. My tongue sticks to the roof of my mouth. My palate feels like sandpaper. I am still feverish. My skin looks like the skin of a very old person, dried up and stiff. Should I give up? It would be so easy. But I have made up my mind—I will not give up. I will tell the world about this inhumanity.

We who lie here dread each advancing day. All know that after a week there is a selection. We speak about it often, we're terrified. Three people, two SS doctors and a prisoner physician, will inexorably decide if a prisoner will be allowed to go on living or die. Those three are lords over life and death. A nod or a wave with a hand from them decides if one is allowed to live or will be transported to the main camp of Auschwitz for gassing. The latter destiny strikes all prisoners who are not able to work, the so-called *Muselmänner*[50] or walking skeletons. They are so skinny that it looks as if their bones are only being held together by their skin.

50 *Muselmann* (pl. *Muselmänner*, or the female equivalent, *Muselweib/Muselweiber*; German for Muslim) was a slang term used by prisoners in Nazi concentration camps to refer to those suffering from a combination of starvation and exhaustion who were resigned to their impending death.

One week passes quickly. Today, I'm up for evaluation by the "board of judgment." My joints ache and my legs are weak after being in a sickbed. I still can't look down at my body, which is unbearably skinny. My head is pounding—it feels like a sledgehammer is banging inside me. I have broken into a nervous sweat. My heart is pounding too and when I try to get out of the bunk, my legs won't carry me. Some friends grab me and lift me forward when 105362 is called. With a little burst of energy, I am on my way toward the judges. I use all my willpower and every ounce of concentration I have to keep myself upright and walk with an even gait toward the table where the three doctors are sitting. Don't think about the pain! I do my best to appear as healthy as possible. I stand for a second before them and then turn around and walk out. I collapse outside the door.

Prisoner number 105362 is on the list to be gassed. The German–Jewish youth leader Artur Posnanski[51] is sitting in the office where the lists are written. He looks at his own number, tattooed on his left arm and realizes that 105362 must be one of the boys who arrived together with him from Berlin. He concluded that this condemned man must be saved. Posnanski switches the number with the number of someone who has just been collected with the other dead. He does this each time he finds a youth who can possibly be saved in such a simple way. He does it six times for me. He fools death six times for me. The Germans don't check the numbers, just the count. Whether a prisoner is dead or alive has no meaning, as long as the count is accurate. *Ordnung muss sein!* (Order is a must!)

Back in my bunk, I am exhausted. Eight days until the next selection. Maybe, just maybe, I will be better by then. My body is worn out from the rheumatism. Pain is my constant companion. Rumors of

51 Artur Posnanski (1912–1998) was a Zionist youth movement activist from Berlin and leading member of the Youth Aliyah movement. He helped organize the departure of Jewish youngsters for Denmark and Sweden in the 1930s. After his deportation to Auschwitz, he became a clerk at the Monowitz office (*Schreibstube*). After having survived the death march from Auschwitz, he was liberated in Buchenwald on April 11, 1945, and later that year he cofounded Kibbutz Buchenwald near Fulda, with the express aim of educating young Jewish survivors for emigration to Mandatory Palestine.

my perseverance have spread. The notorious, Dr. Josef Mengele[52] also hears about me. He is already known for his experiments with live prisoners. Now he has found a new victim—prisoner 105362.

Mengele has a theory that pain will get rid of pain. Therefore, he orders that all my joints are to be injected with 96 percent alcohol. Such a thing has never been tried before. The unfamiliar doctors stand over me with their twenty-one needles. They guide their needles into joint after joint, filling me with alcohol. It stings. It burns. It's like acid. My body arches in pain. I can't lie still in my bed. I can't have a blanket over my body—the weight of it feels like a cover made of iron. I am dying. My entire body is in unbearable pain. From far away I hear my own sobbing. When the night insects make their appearance, and itching takes hold, I pass out.

I am in a bunk by myself. It takes time to recover after the treatment. A long time. Each eighth day there is a selection, but my guardian angel Artur again succeeds in fooling death. A fellow patient sees my weak attempt at walking. He is a French swimming champion and knows how much good massage and light exercise can do. Slowly he gets me back on my feet. I weigh 39 kilograms. My temperature is 34.6 degrees Celsius, pulse 44, and my blood sedimentation rate is 27. In this condition I am taken off the sick list and sent out to work again.

I look terrible. I'm so unbelievably skinny that I don't even recognize my own body. I see my arms and legs move, but don't comprehend that they belong to me. They look like knitting needles. I

52 Dr. Josef Mengele (1911–1979) was a German medical doctor who also held a doctorate in anthropology. From 1940, he served as a physician with the armored Fifth Waffen-SS Panzer (Tank) Division "Wiking," treating many Scandinavian volunteers. After he was wounded, Mengele became a camp physician in Auschwitz-Birkenau, where he conducted often-lethal medical experiments on prisoners, preferably twins, to explore theories concerning genetic inheritance that were considered the basic tenets of Nazi racial theory. He arrived in Auschwitz in May 1943 and continued to serve in the death camp until its evacuation in January 1945. Although he was only one of more than thirty SS physicians in the camp, he became widely known and notorious for his cruelty. After the liberation, he managed to avoid prosecution by escaping to Latin America.

barely manage to make it back to my barrack, which is empty. Everyone is at work. But the SS find something for me to do. I get no extra day to rest here. I fetch bread for all the prisoners in my barrack. I go back and forth many times before all 250 prisoners have received their meager ration. My thin legs swell up and end up looking like wooden posts.

That night I place something under my feet to raise them a little higher, but it doesn't help. The next morning my legs are still very swollen. I report to the *Revier*. The Polish doctor who checks me is not especially willing to admit me into the hospital ward again. I ask him, I beg him, until finally he grants me three more days. Then it's either work again, or a merciless end, he says. Full of gratitude I lie down. The next day I get up at regular intervals and do leg exercises. Both day and night I exercise to reduce the swelling. And it helps! By the third day my legs are functional. Weak, but not swollen.

Although there is neither time nor energy left for friendship, some relationships are maintained. I have not met any other Norwegian prisoners for a long time. I don't know how many of them are still alive. Luckily, however, the Germans whom I met during the transport from Berlin, are with me. We are all between the ages of nineteen and twenty-one. The best years of our youth have been obliterated in this hell. The young Germans are close friends. They help and support one another and often help me, too. We have somehow become united during our time in the camp. In my current state, it's clear to me that I can't walk far. My German friends help me get indoor work, thanks to their connections with the people who assign work duties. I end up in the work detail with the shortest distance to work. It is the IG Farben electrical warehouse.

EIGHT

I report to the Kapo at the electrical warehouse. He asks if I have knowledge about electrical items. I don't think twice about lying, and declare that I worked for Siemens in Trondheim. The work foreman looks doubtfully at me, thinks I look too skinny. But finally nods. I end up in work detail number one. I don't look strong at all. My joints are still painful, but I am alive! Outside it is cold and snowy. As thin as I am it would have been difficult to stay warm. But now I will work indoors without any heavy lifting.

Polish non-Jewish prisoners had been working in the electrical warehouse, but they were sent to Germany to work in a weapons' factory. All German men, including boys from thirteen to fifteen years old, have been called up for military duty at this time. The German defeats are also noticed in the weapons industry. Now Jews in the camp can be lucky enough to get jobs at other places apart from construction sites.

The electrical warehouse is huge. One hundred and sixty meters long and 50 meters wide. It is full of all kinds of electrical items. Thousands of item numbers in German. All order forms are written in Gothic handwriting. It's difficult enough to understand technical terms in German, but handwritten German is impossible for me to read. First, I have to learn what each item is called in German. For many I don't even know the Norwegian name. I try to memorize the names and numbers by heart, then I must learn to decipher the Gothic writing. One of my responsibilities is to maintain the warehouse stock file. These records are stored outside the area of the camp in case of a bomb attack. I develop a method so that only I can decipher what is on the cards. Maybe that will make me indispensable.

The warehouse is not heated, but I have a roof over my head and avoid the wind, snow, and rain. The guards are just as brutal and crude here as they are in other places in the camp. Even though the work detail only consists of 200 men, they scold us no less. If I stand still for a second and ponder what is written on the order form, I quickly hear the Kapo's voice, "Jewish pig, are you lazy? Get to it! Do you think you're at a summer camp?"

Among us are also civilian workers from many occupied countries, both people who have been forcibly drafted and traitors who wish to work for Germany and the Aryan race. But these men live outside the camp. For a while, a young Danish civilian works in the electrical warehouse. We speak a little. He is happy as he will soon be going to Denmark. I ask him to send a postcard home to Trondheim, to Karl Lagerquist, a loyal coworker of our family's firm for the past twenty years. I ask the Dane to tell him that I am alive and that I would like to get a package of food from him. He promises to send a postcard. I tell him my name and prisoner number.

The German soldiers are unbelievably fearful of all forms of infection. They are careful to ensure that every other week, we get clean clothes and a little piece of soap, that we shower and have shaved our entire body. What type of soap it is I don't know, but it isn't like the soap I remember from home. One day, when I receive that little square of soap, I notice there is something in it. I quickly hide the soap as I would be severely punished if it is found. Only in the evening, after I have laid down on my bunk, do I take it out from under the blanket. Here no one can see what I am doing. To my surprise I scrape out a little metal casing. I carefully coax it open. I pull out a 10,000 Reichmark bill. Before the war one could have purchased a small house for such an amount. I look at the bill, confused. What can I use it for? Here, there is nothing to purchase, money has no value. Where did it come from? Maybe someone who hoped to save himself and his family had lost it. Now perhaps it can help me, but how?

I attach the bill behind the prisoner number on my jacket so that it will not be noticed during inspection. I think carefully about how best to use it. For several days I consider how I can use the money to get food. But to whom should I approach about this matter? Civilian Germans, who live outside the camp, also work together with us. I venture forth with a question to an engineer with whom I have a reasonably good relationship. Can he get me food in return for the money? He doesn't promise me anything, but gladly takes the money. During the following days he gets me extra portions of soup. I eat greedily—hunger is a constant ache. You will get more soup, he promises when he sees how happy I am for the extra portions. But unfortunately, he is transferred to another area.

Sergej Kaplan,[53] a Jewish engineer from the Netherlands, is in my work detail. Before the war he worked for the Philips development

53 Sergej Kaplan (1907–?) was an electrical engineer and a head of department at the Philips main plant in Eindhoven, the Netherlands. During the German invasion

department. He built the first electronic shock apparatus for medical use. The SS know this. Dr. Mengele is interested and he wants such an apparatus. Sergej is ordered to build an electric shock apparatus for Mengele. The SS will provide the necessary parts. But they need our help too and an order is given: would the workers of the IG Farben electrical warehouse be so kind as to steal the different components. I must therefore steal from my "employer." As a rule, we undergo a body search when we leave the warehouse, so no one is able to take anything out with them. But the SS have thought about this carefully. Each day we get large pots of soup sent to the warehouse, and before we return them, we must scrub them clean. We must place the ordered stolen items, for example copper wire, in the bottom of the pots. When the pots are brought back to the kitchen, by order of the SS, other prisoners stand at the ready to take the stolen goods to Sergej Kaplan. Eventually, the apparatus is complete.

Dr. Mengele and his staff immediately begin to experiment on male and female prisoners. They want to find out how much electricity a person can bear before he or she dies. It's not enough that the prisoner passes out and goes completely insane from the stress on his or her body. Mengele carries out his experiments on random prisoners, and

his attempt at escaping to England with his wife, Lucy, and their two daughters failed due to the closing of the Dutch ports. When Nazi persecution of the Jews started in the Netherlands, Philips concentrated its Jewish employees in a special research department. In 1943, Sergej Kaplan was taken to the Vught concentration camp, where he was put to work at a special "Philips-Kommando." As more transports were leaving Holland, Sergej and Lucy Kaplan took their daughters to members of the resistance who hid them for the rest of the war, but they themselves were caught as they tried to go underground. On August 24, 1943, Sergej was taken to Auschwitz via Westerbork internment camp in northern Holland. Lucy managed to stay in Westerbork until September 1944, when she was deported to Theresienstadt shortly before the liberation of the Netherlands. From Birkenau, Sergej was sent to Monowitz as a forced laborer. Due to his engineering skills, he joined a group of people led by Polish prisoner-functionaries, who were developing an electroshock device for psychiatric use. The idea for this device was conceived by Polish neurologist Zenon Drohocky (prisoner number 169779) and the group had the express aim of producing this device to please the SS camp physician in Monowitz, Horst Fischer (1912–1966), who was eventually executed as a war criminal.

especially on twins, to find out if one has a different reaction to the other. Ernest Michel,[54] a friend from Berlin, is a medical assistant in Mengele's experimental division. He tells me what takes place, about how doctors drive stronger and stronger electrical currents through the prisoners, such that the body arches in a bow—about how they carry away the unconscious prisoners, never to awaken again.

NINE

October 1944. The Allies are bombing Germany. One city after another is being destroyed. In the distance we can hear the sound of the airplanes. The Allies have gotten wind that Buna Works—the 1,783 buildings of IG Farben's plant—will soon be completed. Germany's production of methanol and rubber will increase, something the Allies must stop at any price.

I stand outside the warehouse. Air-raid sirens are wailing. The Allied planes must be on their way. Everyone is running frenziedly in order to hide. Soldiers and officers seek refuge in air-raid shelters, but prisoners don't have any bunkers in which to hide. I dash into the storehouse to grab my file of index cards, my "work guarantee," turn, and run out at full speed. It happens so quickly that I don't notice the SS man who is speeding toward the air-raid shelter on his Tempo motorcycle. An inferno erupts around me. The sound of falling and exploding bombs—I can neither see, nor hear, anything else. I collide

54 Ernest Wolfgang Michel (1923–2016) experienced Nazi persecution of the Jews in Mannheim, Germany, right from the start. His father owned a cigarette manufacturing business. From 1939 onward, Ernest was sent to several forced labor camps for Jews, and in 1943, he was deported from a camp in Paderborn to Auschwitz. Upon arrival on March 3, 1943, he was selected for Monowitz where his calligraphic skills gained him a position at the *Häftlingskrankenbau* (prisoners' infirmary). Following a death march via Buchenwald to the Berga an der Elster subcamp, he finally escaped from another death march headed for Dachau. After the war, he settled in the U.S. and eventually became vice president of the International Auschwitz Committee.

with *Arbeitsdienstführer* Stolten,[55] who flies off his bike in an arch. The collision was lucky for him. Had we not collided, he would have been blown up by a bomb that fell where his motorcycle would have been. The blast nails us to the ground. The spray of earth falls over us like a tide. Loose things are flying through the air. Despite this, both the SS man and I are still in one piece. But Stolten forgets that as soon as he sees his motorcycle broken into small pieces. Instead of thanking me for the collision, he screams at me while we both try to get to safety. I don't hear anything, I just see his mouth furiously moving.

I carefully feel to see whether all my limbs are still intact. Luckily, I am uninjured. I hold the index-card box tightly and continue to seek shelter from the bombs. A cacophony of sound explodes around me. Bombs and anti-aircraft artillery crackle. Shards of glass fly like projectiles when windows explode. I see that other prisoners are seeking safety behind mixed cement and mounds of earth. The bombers disappear. They have dropped their load, completed their mission. But the noise is still ringing in my ears.

In my mind, I question why the Allies didn't bomb the gas chambers. It would have been so easy. I shrink back, terrified. Is this just a break? Will the planes come back with a new load of bombs? Flames are shooting out everywhere. The air-raid sirens whine "danger over." The survivors come out of their hiding places.

Fortunately, I am not seriously injured. I am bleeding from a slight cut on my skin, but that's all. Slowly I walk across the yard toward the camp and see dead and injured people everywhere. Men shrieking in pain, dying men, men who have gone crazy from the shock. We dig out the dead from under the collapsed buildings and warehouses. Doorways, chairs, tables, beams, iron rods—everything that is found at a construction site—lie intertwined with human body parts.

Sixty-eight Czech and Polish young civilian women are ordered to clean up after the bombardment. Two undetonated bombs lie inside

55 *SS-Oberscharführer* Richard Stolten was a *Blockführer* in the Auschwitz I main camp. In 1941 he was transferred to the Auschwitz III–Monowitz camp where he became *Arbeitsdienstführer* (the leader of labor assignment).

the destroyed storehouse. They surely weigh 250 or 300 kilograms each. The women are commanded to wash the ground and area around the bomb so that German special troops can come in and disarm them. One of my jobs is to ensure that the women fill out their time cards correctly so they can be paid afterward.

This is the first time I have been so close to women since arriving in Auschwitz. But they have no effect on me. I am too weak to think about the opposite sex. I speak a little with the young women, but they are scared of the Germans and fear there will be more bombing attacks. They are cautious about speaking—they cannot shirk their duties. Illness is not a good enough reason to miss work. In spite of this, one of the women is so sick that she asks me to stamp her in and out for a couple of days, just so she can rest and regain her health. I take the chance. To return the favor I ask the girl whether she can get anything for me. She tells me that food isn't possible. Instead, I request some black shoe polish. Black shoe polish! It may seem like an odd request, but it would help me. Hans, who is the Kapo for my work detail, has committed seven murders and is a criminal prisoner. But he is still quite vain. He has managed to get hold of two used uniforms. He had a prisoner, who is a professional tailor, alter them to his size. Now he struts around in an attractive uniform, but with unpolished boots. With my newly acquired shoe polish, I can polish his boots until they shine. I come into favor with the Kapo.

One morning after roll call late in the fall of 1944 I am called into the office of the *Politische Abteilung,*[56] the political department. I am a seasoned prisoner by now and know that it is not a good sign to be summoned there. My heart pounds. The SS has something on

56 The concentration camps under the IKL (Inspectorate of the Concentration Camps) were structured into five departments: 1. *Kommandantur-Stab* (commandant's staff); 2. *Politische Abteilung* (political department); 3. *Schutzhaftlager* (camp administration); 4. *Standortverwaltung* (location of buildings and property); and 5. *Sanitätswesen* (hygiene and medical issues). The political department was subject to the regional Gestapo, not the IKL, and took care of prisoner registration, the interrogation of prisoners, prevention of escape and outside contacts, and combatting any attempts at resistance. Spying against the prisoners—as well as against the SS and other personnel—was also part of its assignment.

me, but what? I rack my brain. What have I done wrong? I know that punishment awaits me. With shaking legs, I go toward the office.

Around the entire camp are two rows of high-voltage barbed-wire fence. Without any explanation, I am commanded to stand between these rows of barbed wire. I stand at attention hour after hour. If I fall forward or backward I will be electrocuted. My body sways slightly toward both sides. I almost fall asleep, but manage to stop myself. I am freezing, it is many degrees below freezing, but I dare not move. The hours pass. The SS guard watches me without compassion. I stand still and wait.

What the hell have I done? There must be a reason for such a punishment. I can't remember having committed a punishable offense. Of course, the SS don't need a reason to punish a prisoner, but nonetheless. They come to get me late in the day and lead me into the guard room. Two SS men stand proudly before me, elegant in their clean uniforms and polished boots. Both of them hold riding whips casually in their hands. They reek of self-confidence. I stand at attention in my striped prison uniform with my hat in my hand. I feel miserable and very small. They ask me how I, a wretched Jew, have managed to contact Norway. I stare incomprehensibly at them. I don't know what they are talking about. One of them raises his whip and strikes my neck. They demand an answer. I shake my head, not knowing what they mean. Then both of them begin to hit me. The lashes hit me systematically over my back, my arms. Suddenly I remember the Danish civilian worker. But I stick with my denial. I dare not go back on what I said. I am ordered to hang from a trapeze bar. One of the SS men lights a cigarette, cursing at me and whipping lashes over me.

"Dirty Jew, you shithead. How the hell have you managed to give your prisoner number to someone?"

The man with the cigarette gets closer. He holds his lit cigarette against my wrists. I scream, lose my grip, and fall toward the stone floor. Confused and beaten, I mumble something about a Danish civil worker with whom I spoke a long time ago. I am close to losing consciousness. The two of them kick me.

"Get up, damned pig!"

After the beating, I'm in intense pain. I drag myself up and they order me to go over to them. I move slowly toward the table, fearful of more blows, and they show me a package in brown paper. It comes from Trondheim. I recognize the neat handwriting of Karl Lagerquist. My name, address, prisoner number. The package has been torn open. I can see a pair of woolen socks, a toothbrush, and a little toothpaste. I'm sure the package was full before. I sway from exhaustion. They order me to take the package and disappear, warning me that if it happens again, I will be a dead man. I leave the office as quickly as I can. I almost have to crawl the last stretch back to the barrack. The open wounds are painful. I clench my jaw and am on the verge of tears. But I don't want to give the torturers the satisfaction of seeing the powerlessness I feel.

Hunger is the worst. It destroys the body and clings to the soul. Weakness is felt in every joint. Hunger drains me of all vitality and destroys my thoughts. Hunger creeps in everywhere, even in my much-needed sleep. Hunger enters my world of dreams. I see a beautifully set table full of food. I know hunger through all the torture and abuse, and it makes me feel faint throughout my workday. My body screams for food. I am unpleasant to look at—clean-shaven over my entire body, a hollow gray face. Food, food, food. Hunger does not release me for even a moment.

During the Jewish holidays someone reminisces about how families gathered together and celebrated Rosh Hashanah (the Jewish New Year), or observed Yom Kippur (the Day of Atonement), which is also a day of fasting. Here, no one is able to fast, though. Here it is necessary to eat every single bit of food you can get. We look like living skeletons. Many prisoners eat everything they come across. Rotten potatoes they find on the ground, moldy bread crusts someone has dropped. One prisoner manages to kill a cat and it turns into a secret feast.

Roll call, work, dead friends, hunger. So go the days and months. Some throw themselves at the electric fence in despair. I see their last convulsions before they become locked in twisted silence. Some go insane and are taken to the gas chambers or shot before our eyes. I see all this, yet I do not see. I do not want to see, I don't want to feel the pain. I drive this kingdom of death before me out of my mind.

My childhood God dies in Auschwitz. To whom should I pray when the pain becomes too much to bear? Who will I believe in when I need help? My friends, fellow prisoners, are the ones I thank for an outstretched hand. Maybe God still exists. But what kind of God sees this hell and does not interfere?

The perpetual noises grind in my ears: the dragging of wooden clogs, the sniffling of eternal colds, the coughing. And the smell that pursues us from the gas chambers and crematorium. All this lies like a yoke around us. I stand in the yard, together with 20,000 other prisoners. We are so skinny that a breath of wind threatens to topple us. We are deadly tired from another day of forced labor and the blows to which we have been subjected. Everyone is freezing. The day has been long and heavy; the Kapo is watching me like a hawk. The SS are at it again. The counting restarts. The numbers don't tally. They yell that someone is missing. I have learned to sleep standing up. I have already seen the gallows that have been erected. Three today! "Let's get it over with," I think. Hunger is screaming. Finally, the counting is complete.

Three very young boys, Hungarian children around thirteen or fourteen years of age, are led forward between heavily armed SS men. One of the boys looks like he is even younger. What kind of crime can these three children have committed against *Der Führer und Das Reich?* The poor kids have stolen some potatoes. Their punishment is hanging. The nooses are placed around their necks. I can't see if they are crying. But I cry. Tears are running down the cheeks of many of us.

"Monsters," I whisper in Norwegian. I don't understand how they can do this.

I have seen friends hanged many times but I have never cried before. I have shut out all elements of caring about others. I would not be able to survive otherwise. This is the first time I cry. These boys are so young. The trapdoor is released and two of them die immediately. But the third is too light. He is slowly asphyxiated. We are dismissed. It is very quiet in our barrack that evening. One prisoner whispers *kaddish,* the Jewish prayer for the dead.

The concentration camp constantly buzzes with rumors. Where they start, no one knows—perhaps from some of the less well-known prisoners, who are said to have radio contact with the Polish resistance, or from some of the civilian workers from the outside who come into Buna Works every morning. Maybe it is simply our own wishes that are voiced? Because this hell cannot continue. Sometimes we can hear muffled sounds in the distance. We reckon they are Allied air attacks. We can now hear these air raids twenty-four hours a day.

The Germans have become more nervous. They are losing more and more soldiers and the SS have also been sent as special troops to the front. The military power hastens to get production under way at Buna Works. We are driven to breaking point to rebuild all that was destroyed following the Allied air attack. Surely it is clear to Hitler and his cronies that the war is lost, but they don't give up. The Nazis don't want the world to discover their industrial mass extermination of the Jews. Therefore, the orders are given to destroy the gas chambers. They are to be blown up! What does that mean? Fear seizes the prisoners. Are they going to kill us all? But the Nazis can't possibly—in such a short time—gas or shoot all the thousands of prisoners in their captivity. The crematorium ovens operate full time, but don't manage to get rid of all the corpses. Now dead prisoners are also being burned outside on pyres. Gasoline is poured over the pyres, a match is lit, 2,000 or 3,000 dead people turn to ash. The smoke from the pyres blends in with the fog and lies everywhere, seeping into us like an internal chill. For miles around, people can't avoid the smell in their nostrils. They know what is happening. But the smell dulls their senses.

In October 1944, the Jews who are working in the *Sonderkommando*, the special command unit, rise to revolt. They are the ones who pull the dead out of the gas chambers, burn them, and dispose of their ashes. They have learned that the SS is going to liquidate them. These prisoners have seen too much. They would be witnesses when Germany capitulates.

Knowing they are condemned to death, the Jews decide to rebel. During the entire war there have been groups of prisoners who have managed to get hold of weapons and hide them. Now, these weapons are to be put to use. On October 7, 1944, the Jewish prisoners destroy the ovens of Crematorium IV. They kill three SS men, and injure others. The heroic prisoners try to flee, but they are quickly surrounded by heavily armed SS guards and are shot on the spot. Two hundred and fifty prisoners are shot during the struggle, and 200 more are shot as punishment and warning. This happens in Birkenau, but it doesn't take long before the whole story reaches us in Buna. We don't know whether we should be happy about the courage displayed by the prisoners in Birkenau, or if we should cry in sorrow that they were killed. But, at any rate, the Germans have incurred a loss and that is good news for us.

TEN

It is the third year in a row that I do not celebrate the coming of the New Year. However, the German SS officers celebrate Christmas. I remember my childhood fun every New Year's Eve, the images pass through my mind. I see the Norwegian flag, the horns we blew, the garlands with which we used to decorate the table, the delicious food. Always enough food. Before me lies the whole year of 1945. Will this year also drown in tones of gray, or is there a small light flickering at the other end of this dark room? Will the war end this year?

Rumor has it that Russian troops are approaching. The SS guards are panicking. Nervousness makes them restless and their commands are fiercer. Their voices, always in crescendo, become shriller. One wave of droning planes after another. The temperature falls. Snow falls. All is dark, hopeless. Depression takes over me. My body becomes heavier. My arms and legs stiffen.

It is the night of January 15, 1945. Silence has sunk into the barrack. I try to fall asleep, but uneasy thoughts spin around in my head. The air-raid siren is sounding. We have nowhere to hide. I remain in my bunk a bit longer. One place is just as good as another. Now bombs are falling over Buna Works. The dark night sky is alight. Many buildings are already on fire. I move slowly toward the door. If a bomb hits the barrack, I will be cooked alive together with all the others. But it is better to be near the exit. There, at least, I have a small chance to get out if a bomb hits the barrack.

Flames shoot toward the winter sky. Anti-aircraft artillery crackle continually. The bombs fall. Fear is in everybody's eyes. Where can we hide from the deadly bombs, from the terrible noise? The uneasiness we feel is like a knife being held against one's throat. Our mouths are dry, hearts hammer, bodies shiver. Someone prays aloud to God. I believe my last hour has come.

But then the unbelievable happens: the frightful night comes to an end and I am still alive. The bombers are gone. Many factory buildings and storehouses are burning, many of them have been blown to pieces. But no bombs hit the camp itself. The quiet is palpable after the night's noise. It takes hours before I can breathe normally again. We are called for morning roll call and I have never been so exhausted. Today there will be no work detail. I am indifferent. I need the day. The cruelty of the previous day consumes me. Together with other prisoners, I wander nervously back and forth outside the barrack. We wonder what will happen now. All kinds of rumors are circulating. The Red Army is getting closer! Germany has capitulated! All prisoners will be eliminated! One rumor has it that we will be taken to Germany. What is true? Time moves at a snail's pace, strangely surreal.

In the evening, the yard is full again. Around 20,000 prisoners. The day has been long. They announce that we will be evacuated tomorrow and that everyone is going on a transport. Then we are dismissed.[57] No one knows more than this. Questions are spinning in

57 Shortly after the Red Army liberated the concentration camp Lublin-Majdanek on July 24, 1944, evacuation transports from Auschwitz and its subcamps began which brought some 65,000 prisoners on transports to other concentration camps. However, thousands succumbed to the horrible conditions and guard violence during the transports. On January 17, 1945, there were 42,000 prisoners in Auschwitz I, Birkenau, and Monowitz. There were another 25,000 prisoners in the remaining Auschwitz subcamps. The 52,000–56,000 who were still able to march were taken on death marches on foot in guarded columns of 1,000–2,500 prisoners. Between January 19 and January 23, the columns reached the Gleiwitz (Gliwice) or Loslau (Wodzisław Śląski) railway stations after 50–60 kilometers in icy, snowy winter weather. Some were sent on to the West in railway wagons, while others were forced to continue for another 200 kilometers on foot to the Gross-Rosen concentration camp (today, Rogoźnica). The total death toll of the evacuation of Auschwitz is estimated at 9,000-15,000 prisoners. As Soviet troops reached Auschwitz on January 27, 1945, they liberated some 7,000-8,500 prisoners in Auschwitz I and Birkenau, and another 800 prisoners in Monowitz, most of whom were seriously ill, along with a large number of unburied corpses.

our heads. Where are we going? How will we be transported? When, exactly, are we going to leave? We don't get any answers, though. And what about all the sick who are lying in the *Revier,* many of whom can't walk on their own? Will they be killed or will the Germans allow them to remain here until the Russians arrive? We try to sleep. We can hear the gunfire from the Red Army in the distance. If only they would come before tomorrow.

But we aren't that lucky. At six o'clock in the morning, there's a roll call, just like any other day. About 20,000 living skeletons are lined up in rows. Each of us has been given an entire loaf of bread, which we hold onto with all our might. Many have thrown a woolen blanket from their bunk over their shoulders to fight off the severe cold. Snow is falling heavily, the wind is whipping furiously. We are lined up five men abreast, 100 men in total per column. March. We walk slowly. It is not until late in the day that more than 50,000 prisoners from the Auschwitz main camp and all the subcamps begin to move. The death march has begun.

We are clothed in striped prison uniforms and have wooden shoes on our feet. Some have lost their shoes and tear pieces of the woolen blankets to wrap around their already frozen feet. We look strange, with blankets over our shoulders, bowls hanging from a knot near our hips, gripping our bread. Our hands are red from the cold. We don't have hair on our heads, just the flat, striped prison hats. We twist through the snow-covered landscape like a gray pile of rags, an endless long snake of people. Many have come from the hospital ward. They dared not remain in the camp. The SS was more likely to shoot them there. They are so weak that they must be supported, their legs alone are not able to carry them. In their faces we read resignation.[58] Our skinny bodies are stooped.

The few Norwegians who are still alive walk with the prisoners of the *Revier.* Herman Sachnowitz marches together with the orchestra. I try to sneak in with the group from the *Revier*, but without success. It is a problem that I don't belong to a small close-knit group. I am just

58 About 7,000 sick prisoners who were not able to leave Auschwitz and the subcamps were liberated by the Russian army on January 27, 1945.

one in the great mass of people. Therefore, I must find a group to join. I talk myself into a group of gardeners. They have a small pushcart in which they have laid their shovels and rakes with the naive belief that the equipment can be of some use where we are going. We are six men walking around the cart as the SS pull us out of the column. Get rid of your cargo! We are ordered to go to the officer's mess to fill the pushcart with cigarettes. We are among the last to leave Buna-Monowitz. Behind us walks a small group of women whom the SS have used as prostitutes. At the very end are armed SS soldiers.

Dusk settles over Auschwitz. This unsightly column of people with clattering wooden shoes drags itself away. The snow whips at us, the wind howls. The SS soldiers encircle the column of prisoners. *Arbeitsdienstführer* Stolten is one of them. He is driving his motorcycle along the rows. He curses and snaps.

"Damn Jews! Wretched slugs! Dregs of the earth!"

Any prisoners who fall he sends to their death with a bullet in their neck. We have started a march with no idea where it will end. Individuals crawl out of the line. They can't take anymore and choose death. One bullet and the torture is over. Quick and painless. Kilometer after kilometer the dead lie strewn in the snow.

Night falls. It becomes colder. I already see frozen corpses along the road. It's true that we are all skinny, but the corpses look even skinnier and smaller in their twisted positions.

"*Los, los*, damned pack! Shitty dogs! *Schneller, los!*"

As if we could walk any faster in our miserable condition! At the edge of the road I suddenly see my friend Leo Eitinger. He looks completely finished, as if he has given up. I lift him up—I don't want him to be shot. I drag him over to the pushcart so he can lean on it. I whisper to him in Norwegian, telling him to hold on, that it can't be much further and that we will survive.

We've got frostbite on our feet, hands, noses, and ears. Our legs are in pain and our thirst is deadly. I open my mouth to catch snowflakes, but it doesn't help. Hunger, the eternal hunger. A continuous moaning sigh climbs up from the column of people, like a wail against God. Before us is only dark and cold, an eternal night. We walk like marionettes. We trample over friends who have stumbled and died. It is almost impossible to pause for even a moment. My eyes are like lead but I dare not close my eyes for even a second. What if I fall asleep? What if I fall? Others will trample over me and I will be gone forever. We walk and walk.

Dawn comes slowly after the long hours of the night.

"*Los, los, schneller!* Damned Jewish pigs, this is no vacation!"

We don't have the strength to move any faster. We have gone far beyond the threshold of pain. We feel nothing. We don't think. We are empty, empty of everything. If you stop to think for one moment, death will come. Friends drop dead. Our legs move automatically. Someone yells that it is time to rest. But our heads don't register the command. We continue walking a short distance further before we stop. We sink down in the snow. We have worn ourselves out during the night. We are beyond exhausted. Luckily, someone wakes me, otherwise I would have never woken up. Even among all these men, I feel completely alone. All each of us can do is watch out for oneself.

We stop near a deserted town. Neither human, nor animal, can be seen or heard. A ghost town. We look around. We are too tired to speak. We get orders to find a place to sleep in the outbuildings of a deserted farm. All rush toward the barn. We lie down wherever we find a spot. Some lie on top of others and are too tired to move. We literally fight over the sleeping spots. Some die from the weight of those who fall over them. I find a place on the floor and close my heavy eyelids. Soon, I am in a deep sleep.

"*Aufstellen!* Line up!"

I wake up stiff, frozen, and coughing, to the yell of this command. I try to move my limbs and get my blood circulation going. Around me I see dead prisoners lying just as they fell. Some are frozen to death, others have been shot. Blood is frozen around the bullet wound. Outside the barn, snow has almost covered the dead, like a soft white blanket. No one does anything to move the corpses. They lie like silent witnesses. Some young boys look for their fathers from whom they were separated the day before. Fathers call for their sons with weak voices. We can't even speak to each other. What would we talk about? Words are inadequate.

"*Los, los! Aufstellen!* We are moving on."

The yell echoes out over the crowd of gray people. The world before us is endless and white. It has stopped snowing, but the snow from the ground is blowing around us, tearing at our faces. It is probably around 5 degrees Celsius. We can feel the cold air deep down in our lungs. The shining stars guide us. Slowly, we begin to walk again.

Far in the distance I see a magnificent house, a mountain hotel. There is light in the window, and smoke rises from the chimney. I want to go there. I'm sure they will take me in. The odd thing is that we never get any closer to the house. It slides over the crest of the hill. My imagination is playing tricks on me. We drag ourselves on, hour after hour. Even more dead are left behind in this icy wasteland.

Stop. We reach Gleiwitz, a deserted camp, surrounded by barbed wire. We have 80 kilometers behind us. Ten thousand prisoners or more have died along the way. The group of gardeners arrives late and all the barracks are overfilled. We are not admitted to a single barrack. One Kapo sees the questions in our eyes—where will we sleep?

His comforting words are, "Dumb Jews, you can lie outside. It doesn't matter anyway."

We look at each other, unable to speak. We are so tired and hungry we almost don't care. Fortunately, we find a window shutter, which we tear off a barrack. It will at least protect us a little against the cold from the stiffly frozen snow. We lie tightly packed next to each other to keep warm. We wake up as the sun throws its first rays up over the frozen landscape. Around me I see hundreds of dead. The cold has taken the life out of them. I am stiff from the cold. It takes time to get onto my feet and get my circulation going again. I hop and jog, but become too tired. I can't believe that I am still alive. I survived last night but I won't survive one more. I have to get indoors.

During the march, I steal some packs of cigarettes. Now I can use them for bartering. I hide them under my prisoner uniform together with a paper bag to use for warmth. I walk around and look into the barracks. Every one is extremely crowded. The Kapos don't want to let me in. In one of the barracks I see a Kapo with whom I have been in contact before. Maybe I can bribe him with cigarettes? It works. He finds a spot for me under the bunks on the floor. Anything is better than lying outside. I crawl in under the low bunk. My body slowly begins to thaw. The warmth from so many people does good. At the same time, the pain in my joints reappears. My feet are swollen and stiff. From my low lair, I can see how people are stepping on both living and dead people who lie on the floor. It's impossible to find a spot to place one's feet without stepping on someone. I can't burden myself with the thought that soon it might be my turn to be trampled to death. I sleep and avoid thinking more about the thirst and hunger that ravage me. We have received neither liquids, nor solids, since we left Auschwitz. The bread was devoured a long time ago. And water is always in short supply. Hunger is driving us crazy.

Thirst makes it almost impossible to even speak. We wander around restlessly. Someone happens upon a storeroom with old bread. We fight like animals to get our hands on this bread. We throw ourselves on one another, scramble over the backs of others to get it. We trample those who fall. We bite and hit. This isn't human. It is a fight for life. The most contemptible side of human nature shows its face. This is pure degradation. I manage to get a loaf of bread. I cling to it and run to my place under the bunks. I carefully eat a little bite of the bread. The rest I hide under my clothes. I dare not eat too much as I don't know when I will get more. My mouth and throat are as dry as sandpaper.

For three days I am locked up here together with all the others. Many collapse, crying and screaming. They use their last reserves of strength to cry. After that, only death awaits. On the fourth morning we hear the familiar yell, "*Los, los! Aufstellen!*"

Again, we stand five in a row, 100 men in each column. It seems that the Germans can only divide by five.

"*Los, los! Schneller,* imbecile Jewish pigs! Assholes!"

The march continues. I don't know how long we walk over the snow-covered plain before we come to some train tracks.

"*Halt, Schweinehunde!*"

We stand straight and are not allowed to sit down. The snow whirls around us. The cold makes me feel sorry for myself. The SS soldiers laugh maliciously when they see some of the prisoners eating snow. The thirst is unbearable. We stare at the railroad track. It seems that we are waiting for a train! Our thoughts are reeling. Is this a good or a bad sign? Where are we going? There is talk of Mauthausen and Buchenwald. If I could choose I would select

Buchenwald. The word Buchenwald (beech forest) sounds like spring and light green trees.

But the most important thing is to join the other Norwegians. I dare not be alone any longer. Everything hurts too much. I feel weak, alone, exhausted. I don't know if I can go on much longer. Carefully, I approach the small group of Norwegians. I position myself next to Sammy Steinmann from Oslo. He belongs to the group from the infirmary. He has been pulling a large trolley of medications since Buna. An SS officer quickly sees that I don't belong here, and chases me away. But I have decided: I will be with the other Norwegians. I steal toward the other side of the trolley where Pelle and Assor Hirsch[59] from Trondheim stand.

"Damn Jew, get away from there!"

The SS officer howls at me. Dejected, I go away and position myself with a group of prisoners who are completely foreign to me. After a while I try again to blend in with the Norwegians. It's finally an advantage to be small. The SS doctor sees me. He sneers at my audacity and stubbornness.

"*Du Jude, bleib stehen, du bist so wie so tot!*" (Jew, just stand here, you are dead anyway!)

The train comes. Open wagons without roofs. The SS soldiers pack us into the wagons. Sixty or more prisoners in each wagon. We stand like an open can of sardines. Luckily, I am together with Leo, Sammy, Assor, and Pelle from Norway now. I don't feel so alone anymore. Again, we are locked in without food or drink. The door is bolted from the outside. I am growing numb, I'm not thinking clearly anymore. I'm standing. I can't fall. I am held up by all the others. It's not easy to get over to the bucket we have in the wagon to relieve oneself. Many don't make it in time.

The train travels through the long, black night. The snow falls on us. I don't feel pain. I am far too cold for anything to hurt. Some die, but are not laid down on the floor. Even the corpses are held upright by the sheer density of prisoners. Only when so many are dead can we

59 Asriel-Berl "Pelle" (1920–1994) and Assor Hirsch (1923–1948). The two sons of Chaim Hirsch (1879–1943) and Marie, née Dworsky (1887–1943) survived

clear a little spot to lay down the corpses. The train moves at a snail's pace. Stopping and starting. It doesn't matter to me anymore. I have no idea how long we have been on the train when someone says something about approaching Prague.

The train stops. We get orders to carry out the dead. They are tossed into a separate car. Now we can sit in our car. The train continues on, stops, then moves again. The thirst is intolerable. Our tongues swell. We open our mouths toward the snowflakes that float down around us. But it barely helps. Some are almost crazy from thirst. One day a pot with watery soup is thrust into the wagon. The soup helps for a few short hours. The next day, some bread is thrown in. We fight to get something to eat. More die. The train stops. We are in Prague. One of the prisoners was born here. He decides to escape. He knows his way around here, knows where he can hide. He persuades a friend to join him. During the night they manage to disappear.

The train continues on. We stand in the open freight cars with dead eyes and dull minds. It is cold, surely well below freezing. We cross the border into Germany. The train stops under a footbridge where a flock of young German boys stand and laugh at the strange train cargo. A prisoner calls to them, asking if they have some food for us. The boys stare at us, then run away. Soon afterward they return with stones, which they throw at us. What kind of youth would throw rocks at starving people in freight cars? How can they behave so spitefully toward us? If we had been animals, they certainly would not have thrown rocks. Are they completely devoid of morals? They cannot possibly avoid seeing that we are suffering humans. But the boys laugh. I am shocked.

The wagon behind us is filled with hundreds of corpses collected from the entire long train. The train journey continues for six days. Days and nights merge together. Now and then the train stands for hours in the same place. I feel myself going steadily downhill. I no longer feel the cold. I no longer know what time of day it is. I am asleep and awake at the same time. At times it is light, at times dark. Now and then I think

the Holocaust, but Assor died in his mid-twenties a few years after the war. Both parents were murdered in Auschwitz, along with their two daughters and three other sons.

that death has claimed me, but the light holds me tightly. I continue to fight to be able to see it. I want to survive!

The train stops. The doors are opened from the outside.

"*Los, los!*"

The familiar words and roars greet us. In our wagon only fifteen men are still alive; six days ago we were sixty. We crawl out. We see from the station sign that we have come to Buchenwald.[60] Fifteen prisoners stand dazedly, dizzy from exhaustion. We note that small numbers of prisoners emerge from the other wagons too.

Why did the SS carry out this transport? What was the purpose of this huge operation? They could have just as easily shot us right away, or simply left us in Auschwitz. These questions are spinning around in my head, but I don't find any rational answer.

ELEVEN

Roll call. Then we drag ourselves in through a new gate, where the words *Jedem das Seine*[61] are written. Buchenwald lies on a hilltop.

60 Buchenwald concentration camp was erected in June 1937 and liberated on April 11, 1945. Located outside the central German city of Weimar, it was one of the largest Nazi concentration camps—by the end of the war, it had become the largest. Around 266,000 prisoners, including 27,000 women, passed through the main camp and its 139 subcamps—including the underground rocket factory Dora-Mittelbau, which became a separate main camp in Autumn 1944 with some forty subcamps of its own. Around 56,000 prisoners died in Buchenwald from exhaustion due to harsh forced labor, starvation, epidemics, as well as guard and Kapo violence; thousands were executed there, too. Buchenwald was also a main location for unethical medical research that killed thousands of prisoners. During 1944–1945, a substantial minority of the prisoners were Jewish, many of whom came to Buchenwald on evacuation transports from Auschwitz. They were generally treated worse than all the other prisoners. At the time of liberation, 21,000 prisoners were still in the main camp, some of whom had armed themselves and attacked SS personnel. In the postwar German Democratic Republic (GDR), the camp resistance rose to legendary status with stories of how the prisoners liberated the camp themselves.

61 *Jedem das Seine* is the German translation of the Latin phrase *Suum cuique* (To each what he deserves), a Bible saying quoted by Martin Luther and other Christian

The trees stand naked and still. The hopeful name doesn't present any beautiful forest. All I feel is the winter cold slamming into me. The same familiar sickening sweet smell, like in Auschwitz, hangs in the air. In the distance I see the chimney from which smoke is rising. There are crematorium ovens here too.

The entrance gate to Buchenwald. Photo Collection, YVA, 6BO1.

The death march and train trip have killed a substantial proportion of the prisoners. We survivors look like living corpses. Our prison uniforms have become even baggier. As always, with arrival to a new camp, we must go through delousing and a complete shaving of our heads and bodies. We must shower and wash ourselves with disinfectant. Our skin is dry with open sores from the lack of food and vitamins. I hate to look down at my body. I almost don't recognize it, and wonder if it will ever be like it was before. I can easily count my ribs. I let my hand slide

church fathers. It was the title of a cantata by the local composer Johann Sebastian Bach, which premiered in 1715 in nearby Weimar. The Nazis took perverse joy in "educating" the inmates of concentration camps in "German culture." The words over the entrance of the Auschwitz I main camp, *Arbeit macht frei* (Work sets you free) is another example of this.

down over my concave stomach. My intestines scream with hunger. My legs barely hold me up, their muscles are weak. My feet have cuts and bruises. There is no mirror here. But by looking at the other prisoners, I know how I must look myself.

We receive clean but thin uniforms. Pants, a jacket, new wooden clogs. Virtual luxuries after the last fourteen days of hell. It is a wonder I am still alive. As this is a new camp we get new prison numbers. My new "name" is 122861. Fortunately, numbers aren't tattooed on us here. Buchenwald has its own system.

We are driven into the *Kleines Lager*,[62] a compound which was originally horse stables. Here there are no beds, only shelves along the walls. Three shelves high. Six or seven prisoners must lie together on one shelf. Here there is no mattress, no blanket, just thousands of prisoners who each must find a place to lie down. Every day, it becomes more crowded. New freight trains continue bringing new prisoners. Everyone eats and sleeps in the same barrack. The air becomes heavy.

There is little rest to be found on the shelf. Many prisoners are sick and are unable to stand up. Nor do they receive the small ladle of soup, that, despite our wretchedness, sustains us a little and is therefore essential to our survival. I laboriously split every crust of bread I get in my hands into several meals. But I never save a single bit, I simply can't. The hunger is tremendous for everyone. When it comes to taking what one can get hold of, moral scruples are nowhere to be found. Therefore, I always carry my bread on me. Even while I walk away from the area of food distribution I keep my eyes open to avoid quick hands reaching out to tear the bread out of my grasp. While I sit on the edge of the shelf, I hear the rattle of death around me. It's as if my surroundings are covered with a veil; everything seems surreal and remote, as if it isn't happening to me.

62 In late 1942, the SS added a separate smaller compound (*Kleines Lager*) to the Buchenwald concentration camp where new arrivals were kept in quarantine before being allowed to enter the larger part of the camp. The 1945 evacuation transports from Auschwitz, and other camps that held many Jewish prisoners, were accommodated in the *Kleines Lager* under unimaginable conditions.

Everything is chaos. No one manages to organize anything. The only way the barrack chief can organize the food distribution is by chasing all the prisoners out of the barrack and then letting us back in one by one. The soup is ladled out in the doorway. Three portions daily. Food distribution takes an endless amount of time, while the cold forces its way into our bodies.

We five Norwegians stick together. But depression takes hold of us; there is not much hope here, nothing to look forward to. There is an unbelievable number of people around me the entire time, all of them on the verge of giving up life. Hungry, exhausted, frozen, skinny men of all ages. Some individuals sit on the ground and eat whatever bugs they find. Their eyes are dead and they are no longer able to keep themselves reasonably clean. They have ceased speaking, only unintelligible sounds come from their mouths. It is so tragic that I almost cannot watch. But in the middle of this confusing melancholy, I try to keep my cool and use the energy I still have in order to survive.

From 1937 until 1941, the camp commander was Koch.[63] When he became the commandant of Majdanek, his wife, Ilse,[64] stayed

63 *SS-Standartenführer* Karl-Otto Koch (1897–1945) joined the SS early, in 1931, and served in leading positions in the concentration camps of Sachsenburg, Esterwegen, Lichtenburg, Dachau, Columbia-Haus (Berlin), Buchenwald, and Majdanek. His reign as a commandant in Buchenwald lasted from 1937–1941. He was relieved of his post due to disciplinary charges of corruption, fraud, embezzlement, drunkenness, sexual offences, and murder. As commandant of Majdanek, negligence was added to the list of charges, when a large group of Soviet prisoners of war managed to escape the camp. In mid-1943, he was transferred to office service at the SS Personnel Main Office in Berlin. In April 1945, he was sentenced to death by an SS court and executed.

64 Margarete Ilse Koch, née Köhler (1906–1967). Married Karl-Otto Koch in 1936. Ilse was appointed *Oberaufseherin* (chief of the small group of female guards) at Buchenwald from 1937 until 1943. She was sentenced to life imprisonment for war crimes in 1951 and committed suicide in jail many years later. The strongly sexualized image of her brutality was widespread among Buchenwald survivors, many of whom had seen a bizarre display of preserved human body parts in the camp shortly after its liberation. The fact that a close SS friend of Ilse Koch had, in fact, collected tattoos from murdered prisoners for his doctoral research

behind in Buchenwald. She was called *Die Bestie*, (the beast), *Die Hexe*, (the witch), or *Die Kommandeuse.*[65] She loved to play the role of the SS. She rode around the camp high up on her horse, enjoying herself on her thoroughbred with a whip in her hand. She has a devilish expression in her almost beautiful face. *Die Bestie* has a bestial hobby. She was said to collect tattooed human skin. If she saw a prisoner with beautiful tattoos, she demanded that they be removed. She was said to make lampshades from the pieces of skin. I wonder what she was thinking when the light shone down on her table.

The winter of 1945 slowly turns to spring. The snow melts. It rains, but it is not warm. Sad gray days are without an end. There are some Norwegian students incarcerated in Buchenwald. They hear rumors that other Norwegians have arrived at the *Kleines Lager*. A couple of students take the chance to come over to the other section of the camp, and smuggle themselves into our barrack. They ask if there are Norwegians here. By coincidence, one of the students knows Sammy Steinmann from Oslo. That becomes our salvation.

As political prisoners, the conditions of the camp are marginally better for the students. They live alone in a barrack, receive Red Cross packages and food from the SS kitchen, and they are not forced to work. The first thing the Norwegian students do is smuggle us five Jewish prisoners into their barrack. They understand how starved we are and there is no end to their generosity. The students shower us with food. And we eat; we get real food and it tastes unbelievably good—heavenly sardines, cheese. We gorge ourselves. The students get hold of warm underwear for us. Just imagine—an end to our frozenness! Our eyes fill with tears of gratitude. My mood improves even more as I recognize

strengthened the accusation. In spite of much contemporary testimony, there was not enough evidence to have her convicted of this extraordinary crime. Most artefacts of the display were lost, and some lamp shades ascribed to Ilse Koch were, in fact, made of animal skin. Flint Whitlock, *The Beasts of Buchenwald* (London: Cable Publishing, 2011) describes the Kochs' atrocities in depressing detail without presenting conclusive evidence on the most extreme accusations.

65 The German word *Kommandeuse* means a female commander, the wife of a commander, or a bossy woman. Prisoners and SS who used the nickname were most likely referring to all meanings of the word.

three students from Trondheim. My old friends Kjell Holmen,[66] Petter Andreas Claussen,[67] and Carl Johan Breida.[68]

The first night after our frenzied eating I wake up in the barrack convinced that I have dreamed the whole thing, that my imagination must have played a trick on me. I understand it is no dream, though. I am still hungry, that's true, but not as hungry as I have been on previous nights. I sit up on the shelf in disbelief that I have spoken with other Norwegians, and I have had ordinary food. Then I go back to sleep again.

Somehow the students manage to get us moved into the main camp, which is not as overcrowded as the *Kleines Lager*. Right away, our existence is much easier. There are 512 Norwegians in the camp. Now and then we sneak over to them, get a little extra food and vitamins, speak Norwegian, and dream about Norway. I am easily moved—a hug or some nice words are enough. The students play chess and bridge, they

66 Kjell Holmen was a law student, arrested on November 30, 1943, and deported to Buchenwald on January 14, 1944. Apart from two months at a subcamp of Natzweiler-Struthof—the SS training camp Sennheim in Cernay (Alsace)—he was in Buchenwald until March 5, 1945, when he was transferred to the so-called Scandinavian part of Neuengamme concentration camp near Hamburg and evacuated by the Danish and Swedish Red Cross "White Buses" to Sweden in April 1945.

67 Petter Andreas Claussen (1920–1984) was a law student, arrested on October 17, 1943, and incarcerated in the Bredtveit prison and the Berg internment camp. In December 1944, he was deported to Sennheim and shortly after to Buchenwald. From there, he was transferred to Neuengamme concentration camp in March 1945 and then evacuated to Sweden. In postwar Norway he took on the law firm his father had founded with a partner.

68 Carl Johan Breida (1923–2001) was a Norwegian secret agent who was trained in England by the Secret Intelligence Service (SIS) and airdropped in October 1944 together with Tormod Morset (1920–1997) over the Gauldalsfjellene mountains, south of his native Trondheim. From a secret observation post, they radio transmitted intelligence reports to London about German ship and train transports entering and leaving Trondheim. After his arrest in early 1945, Breida was sent to Buchenwald. He was evacuated via Neuengamme. The son of a Trondheim banker, Carl and his family later emigrated to Canada, where he worked as a financial analyst in Toronto.

read and treat others well. The belief that we five Jews—Leo Eitinger, Pelle and Assor Hirsch, Sammy Steinmann, and I—will survive and return to Norway is alive again.

For the most part, Buchenwald contains political prisoners who wear red triangles and are mostly not Jewish. There are representatives from different opposition groups—the Labor Party, Communists, and other enemies of Nazi Germany. In Buchenwald, the Communists hold the power among the prisoners, as opposed to Auschwitz, where criminal prisoners with green triangles were the power holders among the prisoners. In Buchenwald, brutality between the prisoners is not as savage and harsh. Intellectual and politically strong prisoners have managed to organize the camp much better than in Auschwitz. Many of the prisoners have been imprisoned in Nazi concentration camps since 1933–1934, from just after Hitler came to power. We hear about Göring's factories, the Gustloff Works,[69] which lies right outside the camp. Prisoners worked there and produced weapons. But the factories were bombed and destroyed in August 1944. Some prisoners were able to smuggle weapons into the camp, though; these are hidden in the potato cellar for future use.

Many newly arrived prisoners pace aimlessly back and forth between the barracks. Assor, Pelle, Sammy, and I are placed in a work

69 The Wilhelm-Gustloff-Stiftung, founded in 1933 in order to capitalize on confiscated Jewish property, manufactured pistols, rifles, machine guns, and light artillery weapons. In March 1943 it established a rifle factory, adjacent to the Buchenwald concentration camp, which mainly used prisoners as its workforce. The SS wanted to strengthen its economy and place the prisoners at the disposal of German industry without losing control of them. However, Heinrich Himmler's concept of *KZ-Betriebe* (concentration camp factories) met resistance from Albert Speer's Ministry of Armaments and from German industry, so from 1943–1944 onward, instead of converting the main concentration camps into major armaments centers, large numbers of concentration camp prisoners were sent into existing factories, which became subcamps near their facilities. The SS remained in charge of the prisoners and was paid a daily fee by the companies for their forced labor. Wilhelm-Gustloff-Werke II in Buchenwald was an early *KZ-Betrieb,* and the concentration camp forced laborers never reached a level of productivity that was anywhere close to that of free, voluntary workers. To the rank-and-file SS, the idea of "work-as-punishment" or "annihilation by work" always took priority over "rational" exploitation of prisoner labor.

detail that is sent to the woods to fell timber. Leo, who is a trained physician, gets work in the *Revier*. Heavy work in the woods is better than having time for heavy brooding, in any case. When I walk in the woods, I think about the required civil duty in which I took part in Hølonda (near Trondheim) in 1941.[70] There, I learned how to fell a tree. The Buchenwald Kapos do not know how to do this. Beech is a hard type of tree, and we don't have anything to help us besides an ax, a saw, and our own manpower.

We work together in teams of two. Hundreds of these teams are spread across the woods. Almost all are equally unskilled, barely even knowing which way a tree will fall. So, it happens more than once that a tree falls on a prisoner. Our strength is nothing to brag about. Occasionally the ax slips and cuts a hand or foot. Many are seriously injured, losing a finger or damaging a tendon. When the tree finally lies on the ground, we lop off the branches and carry the tree over to the forest road. Fifteen to twenty men are needed to carry this heavy load. Many don't have the strength and collapse under the strain. We Norwegian Jews are lucky. The extra food we get from the students gives us renewed strength.

One day twenty of us are gathered to move a tree trunk over to the forest road. It is heavy, but we must get it up on our shoulders.

"*Eins, zwei, drei*..."

The Kapo bellows. But we cannot lift it, and the tree falls on the ground. He screams that we are damn idiots. The man standing right next to me isn't able to jump away. The tree trunk hits his leg. His leg is broken, splinters stick out of the wound, blood splatters. We struggle to get the heavy trunk off him. But it is too late. He dies before our eyes. Again, we get the order to carry the tree trunk to the forest road. Our dead companion is left behind. Many friends are hurt here in the woods. Backs and legs give out, the food ration has become even

70 In the summer of 1940, the Norwegian central administration established a voluntary labor service (Arbeidstjeneste, AT) which placed young men at the disposal of construction, farming, and forestry projects. From September 1940, it was taken over by the Norwegian Nazi party and reorganized along paramilitary lines. From 1941 onward, service in the AT became mandatory for young Norwegian men of military age.

smaller, and after years in the camps, strength is being sucked out of the body.

Every day we hear the distant sound of Allied planes. The air-raid siren sounds strong and steady. The SS soldiers run into the camp. They have realized that the bombs don't fall where the prisoners are held. On the other hand, outside the camp the bombs can fall close to each other. We see ordinary SS soldiers being sent away to the front. Older Wehrmacht soldiers are now dressed in SS uniforms. But these soldiers aren't of the same coarse caliber, not nearly as brutal. The Norwegian students remind us of the value of friendship, of consideration for each other. We begin to gain weight and after a while, we look considerably better. Our strength is returning, albeit slowly, and with it, optimism and the will to live.

One evening in March 1945, Sammy and I con our way into the Norwegian barrack. Inside, we notice an atmosphere of anticipation. The students are happy and tell us that all Norwegian and Danish prisoners are going home. A special envoy from Sweden, Count Folke Bernadotte,[71] is coming to get all Scandinavians. We ask, again and again, whether it's true. We cannot believe what we are hearing. The student leader gives us instructions to pass on the information to all the Norwegians in the Jewish barrack. We will meet in their yard while the others are at their worksites the next day. We rush back to our three friends and tell them the unbelievable news.

I sleep quite poorly that night. My excitement cannot be contained. Home, home, I sing inside my head. In the morning we give the little extra food supply and the extra clothes we had received from the students to our fellow prisoners who are not lucky enough to be able to leave the camp. After the morning roll call, none of the Norwegian Jews go to their work detail. We steal into the yard and

71 Folke Bernadotte (1895–1948) was a member of the Swedish royal family, a diplomat, and envoy of the Swedish Red Cross. In 1945, he joined an ongoing Danish-Norwegian rescue operation and obtained the release of thousands of additional prisoners from Nazi concentration camps by negotiating with SS chief Heinrich Himmler who was hoping to obtain a partial peace agreement with the Western Allies so that they would join forces with Nazi Germany against the Soviet Union.

stand together with the Norwegian students and Danish political prisoners. The wait seems so long as is always the case when one is looking forward to something. I don't know for how long we stand there, but it feels like hours.

Then, a Norwegian student leader walks over to us. He tells us that we five Jews have been struck from the list for transport. We stare at him in disbelief and ask him what he means by this, why we have been struck from the list. He explains that he doesn't know but that he received orders from their leader to give us this message. He also says that if any problems occur after their departure, we should bring them and ourselves to the attention of Julius Jürgensen[72] or Willi Grünert[73] in Barrack 44. They will help us. We are told that Jürgensen speaks Danish and he is originally from Kiel. He knows how to take care of things. They wish us luck, and with that, the student leader is gone.

Never in my life have I felt so forsaken. Am I not Norwegian? I was born in Trondheim, went to a Norwegian school, am a Norwegian

72 Julius Jürgensen (1896–1957) was born in Flensburg on the German–Danish border. He was a factory worker who became a leading regional politician for the German Communist Party (KPD). After his incarceration by the Nazis, he emigrated to Denmark in 1935 where he secretly helped to survey the German refugees. In 1937, he volunteered to fight in the republican forces in the Spanish Civil War. After the defeat of the Spanish Republic, he was interned in southern France and in 1943 he was handed over to Nazi Germany. From January 1944, Jürgensen was a prisoner at Buchenwald. After the liberation he was instrumental in reestablishing the KPD in Hamburg and Schleswig-Holstein. After the ban of the party in 1957, he settled in the German Democratic Republic and became a member of the ruling Socialist Unity Party (SED).

73 Willi Grünert (1901–1985) grew up in Berlin and Kiel and participated in the Sailors' Uprising in Kiel in November 1918. He joined the Communist Party, worked as a labor organizer, and emigrated in 1935 to Denmark from where he was later extradited to Germany. In 1941, he was sent to prison, and to Buchenwald in 1943. There he became a leading member of the clandestine resistance organization. After the liberation, he was active in reorganizing the KPD in Hamburg and Schleswig-Holstein. In the early 1950s, he settled in the GDR and became the leader of the International Seamen's Club in East Germany's largest harbor city, Rostock, assisting—and spying on—visiting sailors.

citizen. Who am I if I am not Norwegian? Am I just prisoner number 105362 or my new Buchenwald number, 122861? It is as if I have been hit over the head. My entire identity is suddenly gone. I have lost everything—Pappa when I was eleven, Mamma and my brother in Auschwitz, together with most of my relatives. I am twenty years old and have spent the best years of my youth in concentration camps. Are Norwegian Jews not Norwegian?

After the Norwegian students leave, the loneliness feels deadly. Are we Jews forgotten? Are we really below humanity, exactly what the Germans want us to be? We five are left standing empty and infinitely miserable, grief-stricken, and alone. But we are still alive. We are Norwegian, Jewish men and now we have only each other to rely on. We must go to work again, back to barrack life, to misery.

The beech trees stand light green and beautiful in the cold sunlight. Spring has come. The earth is thawing and the forest floor sends out a delightful earthy smell. Sammy and I are lucky. We must chop the tree trunks into briquettes. Charcoal is used as fuel for cars, the wartime gasoline. Sammy tells me about his mother who died before the war and his brother Harry who perished in Auschwitz. He knows that his father and other siblings saved themselves by crossing the border to Sweden. We speak about the dreams we carry with us—about Norwegian snow, food, the celebrations of May 17,[74] Jewish family celebrations like Rosh Hashanah (the Jewish New Year), Pesach with matzah (the unleavened bread), and Succoth with our festive outdoor temporary huts. We speak about the Sabbath; its smell, the candles, our mothers' delightful challah (the special braided bread), and about families who perhaps survived. We talk to stay warm and we can almost taste the food in our mouths. But we dare not open ourselves to grief. Instead, we dream about freedom, about returning home to Norway. We understand what happy childhoods we have had, in spite of Sammy

74 The Norwegian National Day. On May 17, 1814, the first democratic constitution was decided by the National Assembly at Eidsvoll Manor, institutionalizing the sovereignty of Norway, which had been under Danish rule for centuries. The day is celebrated by processions and festive events all over the country and among Norwegians abroad. Many dress up in folk costumes on this day.

losing his mother and I losing Pappa. We come from good families, with tight bonds and strong Jewish traditions. We know that it is possible to survive this hell.

The spring sun is shining. The bright morning makes everything easier, even though the five of us have become horribly disillusioned by the students' departure. The drone of the Allied planes washes over Buchenwald. The air-raid siren sounds many times every day. We seek shelter where we can find it and hope that the bombs won't hit us now either. But the Allies' target is not Buchenwald. Their target is industrial areas elsewhere.

It is April 3, a Tuesday. The SS commander informs us over the loudspeaker that American troops are making their way toward the camp. The prisoners will not work any longer. The camp shall be surrendered in an orderly military manner.

On Wednesday, April 4, the next order comes.

"*Sämtliche Juden auf den Appellplatz antreten!*" (All Jews report to the yard!)

We look at one another. What does this mean? Why just Jews? Are they going to kill us and fulfill Hitler's dream of cleansing the world of all Jews? Is this the "Final Solution" for us? Such an order is an indication to seasoned prisoners that something is wrong. Orders for Jews only are not a good sign. We decide not to report to the yard and remember the students' advice to seek the help of the Communist leader Julius Jürgensen. He immediately understands the situation and hides us in the loft of their barrack. He has already hidden some other prisoners there. Leo is not with us. He is hiding in the infirmary. The Jews that report to the yard are taken on a "transport." It is a short trip. Just outside the camp, they are mowed down by a spray of bullets from the SS soldiers.

Jürgensen and his friends tell us what happened to those who were sent on the "transport." They ask us to be as quiet as possible in the loft. We have to stay there. No one knows what the SS will do. The Communists are well informed and are counting on the American liberation of the camp very soon. Rumors have it that General Patton is with his army near Erfurt, which is about 20 kilometers from Buchenwald.

There are more Jews who try to hide. Under mattresses, under beds—wherever one can find a hiding place. But the SS discover the Jews and begin a systematic hunt for them. Barrack after barrack is searched. All Jews who are found are sent on a "transport." The manhunt continues day after day while we lie still in the loft. Jürgensen, Grünert, and their friends provide food for us and keep us informed about what is happening.

When the SS believe that all the Jews have been caught, the search for the criminals—those with the green triangles—begins. The eternal power struggle between them and the political prisoners (those with red triangles) ends to the disadvantage of the criminals. The Russian prisoners of war are the SS soldiers' next victims, then the sick from the *Revier*. All are sent on "transports"—to death. The SS officers follow Berlin's orders of *volle Vernichtung* (total annihilation).[75]

After three or four days we venture out from our hiding place. We tear the badges off dead non-Jewish prisoners and sew them onto our clothes. New prisoner numbers will make it difficult to identify us as Jews. The SS are now in a complete frenzy. They are uncertain about what is going to happen. Jürgensen orders us to remain inside the barrack. What matters now is to stay alive until the Americans arrive.

On April 11, we hear shots in several places around the camp. Then all is strangely quiet. I sit with some other prisoners around a table

75 On April 14, 1945, after the liberation of Buchenwald, Heinrich Himmler issued a general order to the camp commandants that no concentration camp and no single concentration camp inmate must fall into the hands of the Allies. The prisoners were to be taken to safe locations in order to continue working as forced laborers for the Reich. From mid-1944 onward, Himmler and other leading administrators of the concentration camp system issued several contradictory orders: should the camps be handed over to the approaching Allied forces or be liquidated after evacuation of the prisoners, or should they be destroyed by fire or explosives after the killing of the prisoners? However, the legend of a general order, to annihilate all concentration camp inmates, quickly became part of the folklore of camp survivors. See Stanislav Zámečník, "Kein Häftling darf lebend in die Hände des Feindes Fallen. Zur Existenz des Himmler-Befehls vom 14–18 April 1945," *Dachauer Hefte,* 1 (1985), p. 219.

in the barrack. We peer out the window and try to form a picture of what is happening. All of a sudden, I notice that a white flag is being raised over the guard tower.

I stand up and yell, "Look, a white flag! We are free, free...."

Free. The word sings inside of me. I turn toward a German political prisoner who has been in concentration camps since 1933. The little unassuming Berlin man collapses before my eyes. Several prisoners rush to help him. He is having difficulty breathing from the shock of happiness. We carry him over to a cot. Someone gets water. We hold his hand, speak to him encouragingly. But the shock is too great and he dies. For twelve years, he has fought to survive this hell, and in the moment of liberation he died of joy.

We are free. The word alone is beautiful. But suddenly I don't know what to do with my freedom. It feels overwhelming. Uniformed American soldiers enter the camp, telling us that we are free now. I run to them as if I am intoxicated. The frightened faces of the soldiers convey more than words what a shock they have received by seeing our appearance.

At this moment of liberation, 21,400 prisoners are still alive. Eight days earlier the count was 65,000. A total of 43,600 people, old and young, are gone. Ten thousand were mowed down in the course of the last few days. They lie in mass graves outside the camp. The rest have been sent on "transports" to other camps.

We are jubilant and embrace one another, crying, laughing, free, free, free.... We can't say the word often enough. It is too unbelievable to be true. Most of the Americans must continue toward Berlin. We get orders to bring out the hidden weapons from the potato cellar. The leaders are now the German Communists, Julius Jürgensen and Willi Grünert. The prisoners take over the posts of the SS guards. Everything must be done properly. No one can leave or enter the camp without a permit. We will make sure that no SS soldiers sneak into the camp and disguise themselves as prisoners in stolen prison clothes. Several have tried this trick in the past few confusing days. Now we will guard the SS, and we will do it well.

The American soldiers in the camp shower us with gifts. Cigarettes, chocolate, food. It is heaven. One day a few of us are sent 8

Julius Paltiel and fellow Norwegians in Buchenwald on April 17, 1945. From left to right: Leo Eitinger, Assor Hirsch, Sammy Steinmann, Julius Paltiel, and Pelle Hirsch. Courtesy of the Jewish Museum, Trondheim.

kilometers away to Weimar on an assignment. Among the inhabitants, we suddenly see a familiar face, an *Arbeitsdienstführer* in civilian clothing. We take great pleasure in arresting him. We order him to run. It's one of the best things that I have ever experienced.

"*Los! Los*, you pig. Faster, this is no vacation!"

We hand him over to the American officer who quickly throws him into solitary confinement. Unfortunately, the Nazi is able to commit suicide.

All the water in the camp is gone. The SS has damaged the water main from Weimar. The American commander, Captain Peter Ball,[76] is furious. If the water pipe is not fixed immediately, the inhabitants of Weimar will carry water to the camp. Meanwhile, the Americans make arrangements to transport water in tanker trucks.

76 Peter Ball (1913–2006) was a U.S. army captain, and part of the United Nations Relief and Rehabilitation Administration (UNRRA). After liberation, he commanded Buchenwald and other former concentration camps and won the U.S. Legion of Merit honor for his work with displaced persons.

The inhabitants of Weimar, young and old alike, are now ordered to go to Buchenwald. They must see the camp they claim they knew nothing about. It is a shocking experience for them to see how we have been living. They are confronted with *Muselmänner* and instruments of torture.

On April 12, Leiv Kreyberg[77] from Bergen, in my home country, arrives at the camp. He is a diplomatic observer for the American army and takes part in the advance toward the front line. Kreyberg meets with us five Norwegians. He promises to notify the Norwegian government-in-exile in London that we are alive and that we would like to go home in order to fight against the Germans in Norway. In the excitement of being liberated, I cannot allow myself to forget that Norway is still at war. The Germans have only capitulated in those places where the Allies are now present.

On one of the warm spring days in which we wander restlessly between the barracks and the roll-call yard, we speak about how long we will have to remain here. And what will we find when we return home? Suddenly a voice cuts through the camp loudspeaker system.

"*Er det noen nordmenn i denne leiren?*" (Are there any Norwegians in this camp?)

We are requested to proceed to the gate. Is it possible? Was the voice over the loudspeaker Norwegian? We move toward the camp gate. A man approaches, wearing the uniform of an American officer. He hesitates, then walks toward me.

"Is that you, Doddi?"

I stare at him. Who is he? I can't see the face, which is covered by a large helmet. It's only at home in Trondheim that anyone calls me Doddi. Before I fully comprehend what is happening, the man in the American uniform has me in a bear hug. Now I know his voice. It is my cousin, Josef Mendelsohn,[78] who fled to the U.S. when the war

77 Dr. Leiv Kreyberg (1896–1984) was a Norwegian pathologist, professor at the University of Oslo from 1938 until 1964, and helped organize the medical service of the Norwegian army.

78 Josef Mendelsohn (1916–1992), son of Aron and Thora Mendelsohn. He grew up in an Orthodox Jewish household in Trondheim, studied engineering at the Norwegian Institute of Technology, and played the violin in the university orchestra.

broke out in Europe. Now he's a soldier in the U.S. army. We cry and laugh, clinging to each other. It feels so incredible to see my own cousin here after so many years. Tears run freely. We sit down on the ground and talk. The feelings are so overwhelming and it's difficult to find the right words. But I try to tell him about everything that has happened, about all those who are gone—including his own parents and eldest brother, Mamma, Idar, and many others. These are emotional hours for us.

It feels good to see Josef. It's as if a part of my childhood is alive again. I am a human, and there is someone who cares about me. Josef tells me that he has been to many concentration camps looking for his parents, brother, or other family members, but to no avail. Now he knows the truth. He is shaken, but at the same time happy to see me and my Norwegian friends. We are the first Norwegians he has met in the camps. Josef is shocked about the conditions in the camps—the dehumanization to which the prisoners have been subjected.

After a couple of days, Josef returns with toothbrushes, shaving equipment, real soap, chocolate, cigarettes. It is good to feel like a human being again. Josef and I speak about the war, which still rages in many places, and commiserate that we can't fight against the Germans in Norway. He has given me Camel cigarettes, which I smoke. I offer him one, but he shakes his head.

"No thanks, that's not my brand."

I look at him not really understanding what he means by this. But I see the smile in his warm eyes. We both burst out laughing. The answer is incomprehensible to me after having lived for several years without any kind of choice. He understands my reaction. Imagine! To be able to choose what I want again! It is so unbelievable. I must pinch myself several times a day, you cannot imagine how it feels.

Upon graduation in 1939, he moved to the U.S. in order to continue his studies. In 1943, he volunteered for the U.S. army and joined a Norwegian battalion fighting in central Germany. After liberation, Josef Mendelsohn visited several concentration camps in search of Norwegian survivors.

Julius Paltiel with his cousin Josef Mendelsohn and fellow Norwegians in Buchenwald after liberation. From left to right: Pelle Hirsch, Samuel Steinmann, Josef Mendelsohn, Julius Paltiel, Leo Eitinger, and Assor Hirsch. Courtesy of the Jewish Museum, Trondheim.

We speak with many American soldiers. A Norwegian–American is specifically looking for Norwegians. His name is Sivert Stakland.[79] His family comes from Stokland outside of Bergen. He does everything he can to help us, even gets us clothes from the American military stores. It is glorious to see oneself in a new uniform. Our bodies are still skinny but at least now we have clean, thick clothes with which to warm them. I become Sivert's assistant and travel with him to Jena where the American troops have their warehouse. I see the soldiers throw away tins of bacon just because there are some small holes in the packaging. I ask if I can have the cans. Of course I get them. I hide them for later.

One day when I go out into the yard, there is a big commotion. A man is being beaten and kicked by some Belgians who were prisoners until liberation. I am told that this man, this "pig" has dressed like a prisoner and has hidden among us. I am told that he is one of the worst

79 Sivert Daniel Stakland (1882–1949) was a Norwegian ship charterer.

tormentors, a traitor from Belgium. Many kick the man, others stand and enjoy the sight of the degradation he is experiencing. I think about all the pain the man has caused to his fellow citizens. I get into position and kick him in the side with all my strength. It feels good. That single kick is enough. Something relaxes inside of me. All my aggression, all my hate, disappear with that kick. I feel lighter. I feel like a new man. I look at the man with disdain before I turn away. After that experience I am no longer obsessed with punishing the executioners.

May 1, 1945, a beautiful spring day in Buchenwald. The forest stands in glorious bloom—the bright branches of beech trees, the warmth of the forest floor, small flowers peeking up. On that day, there is to be a huge freedom gathering. We manage to sew a Norwegian flag from different scraps of clothing we have gathered. I get the honor of carrying that beautiful Norwegian symbol at this peace celebration. Officers from the Russian and U.S. forces give speeches. Music is played. We stand under a Norwegian flag. We cry from joy, but also in pain that freedom has not yet come to Norway.

At this moment, 21,400 liberated prisoners sing their national songs. This is one of the few good memories I can take home with me from this hell on earth. A brotherhood of nations.

PART THREE

HOMEWARD

ONE

Where is the Norwegian liaison officer? We don't want to stay here any longer. We are impatient. Official helpers from other lands arrived some time ago to assist their citizens. But it doesn't look like anyone is coming for us. Cousin Josef in the U.S. army has told his boss my story. His boss invites me to come along with his battalion to the U.S., but I want to go home to my homeland Norway.

The Americans still take care of us. Food and water, cigarettes, coffee, we get all of this in abundance. Considering our circumstances, we have it quite good. But now we really want to go home. A radio is installed in the camp and each day former prisoners from all different countries and political opinions gather to hear the news of the German capitulation. We revel together when the Germans surrender in Italy, Austria, the rest of Germany, Denmark, and finally in Norway.

"Norway is free! I want to go home!" I yell, and am followed by my four Norwegian friends.

We decide to speak to a friend from Belgium. Maybe he can speak with his liaison officer about getting us *Ausweise* (exit visas), so that we can leave the camp. While we wait for an answer, we check all the barracks to see if there are any more Norwegians here, someone whom we don't know about. We go from barrack to barrack and find Alf Knudsen[80] from Lillesand. He had been unable to leave together with the Norwegian students. At that time, he was in the *Revier* with typhoid fever. Now he is well again. But we see how skinny he is and begin with a course of treatment to help him gain weight. He needs more strength to be able to travel home with us.

The Belgian liaison officer orders exit visas for us all. The next problem is getting transportation from the camp. Sivert Stakland toils to help us. Through a chance visit to the camp, Captain Goddall, a chaplain of the Allied forces on his way to Berlin, gets us a ride with a driver of a German ambulance that had been confiscated by the Americans. With the armor-plating draped in a Norwegian flag, we are driven all the way to Kiel in the ambulance.

The German cities are a horrific sight. The Allied bombs have caused incomprehensible damage. We don't feel any great sorrow over the destruction and the ruins. But we don't feel joy either. In any case, nothing can take away the joy over our freedom. The feeling is indescribable and the splendid spring weather makes the days perfect. I cannot help but see the terrible losses that ordinary Germans have suffered, but at the end of the day, most of them chose freely to support Adolf Hitler—made him their *Führer*. I am one of many millions of innocent sacrifices created by the Nazis' misdeeds. Many Germans are walking around aimlessly in threadbare clothes, amid the ruins of bombed-out buildings. Are they searching for their

80 Alf Knudsen (1920–2017) was a sailor in the Norwegian merchant navy and a resistance activist. In February 1943, he was arrested and tortured at the Gestapo regional headquarters of Kristiansand. He was taken to Grini concentration camp and on December 8, 1943, he was deported to Germany aboard the SS *Monte Rosa* via Århus in Denmark. From February 1944, he was a prisoner of the Natzweiler-Struthof concentration camp in German-occupied Alsace. In September 1944, as the Allies drew close, he was transferred to Dachau, was subjected to forced labor in the Dachau subcamps, and was in Buchenwald at the end of the war.

belongings? They barely notice us as we drive by. Their eyes wander. It's as if they don't want to look at us, like they want to hide themselves. We speak about the fact that it is mostly older women and children we see.

The road is in poor condition—bombed to pieces, destroyed by heavy military vehicles. But the Allies have laid provisional bridges over the worst craters in the road, so, in spite of the destruction, it is relatively easy to pass through. Some city streets actually appear quite normal, until we discover that only the facades of buildings are intact. The rest is leveled to the ground. Among the ruins, a single church spire rises, an unbelievably beautiful sight from a bygone age. Near Kiel we are stopped by the British military. We have now driven into a British zone. Our German ambulance is not allowed to cross this border. It is still a German vehicle, even though the Americans have taken it for their own use.

We are standing in the middle of Kiel with our motley collection of things—my two cans of bacon and a Norwegian flag. It is the afternoon of May 16. Our goal is to get to Free Denmark by May 17, the Norwegian Independence Day. We ask three British officers about transportation to Flensburg. They don't have the authority to get us a car, but they bring us a can of gasoline, which we readily agree to take. Luckily a large truck stops. The driver is willing to take us to his military camp. He is also a former camp prisoner and says maybe we can get help in the military camp.

We get off the truck outside the canteen and are told to wait until the British officers have had their afternoon tea. Time passes. We wander impatiently back and forth. We so much want to celebrate May 17 in Denmark tomorrow. Four or five British officers immaculately dressed in uniform leave the canteen, each with his little officer stick under his arm. We greet them politely, and I show them my exit visa from Buchenwald. It says I am a prisoner from Auschwitz and Buchenwald, but I was born in Trondheim. One of the officers asks me whether I'm really from Trondheim. When I reply that I am, he asks me if I know a family named Sundet. I look at the officer, smile, and tell him that when we lived on Bergsligaten, I had a friend named Sundet whose father was a fish wholesaler. The officer can't believe it; the father is his uncle! He is overjoyed.

The world is a small place. In the middle of this bombed-out land, I meet a Canadian–British officer, who by chance asks me, a resident of Trondheim and a concentration camp survivor, about someone from Trondheim, and I know this person. This meeting is the salvation for our continued journey. The officer quickly feels responsible for us and promises to do what he can to help.

We are attended to in the former SS canteen, and get instructions to take it easy until the next day. The officer will arrange a ride for us, one way or another. We can spend the night here. Outside the canteen we can smell lilacs, which we take inside for decoration. There are no beds here. We tip over some cabinets and lie down on the veneer wood on the backs of the cabinets. For us they are grand beds. The officer comes in with a bottle of whisky and admires the Norwegian flag we have hung up between the branches of lilacs. We are full and a little drunk. This is our first real celebration in many years.

The next morning, Sundet's nephew finds us a little Opel Kadett and a former prisoner, a huge Russian, to be our driver. The car is so overloaded, we sit on top of each other. After a few kilometers one of our tires has a puncture. But as luck would have it, there's a garage not too far away. My two tins of bacon come in handy and we get a new tire, which is mounted in record time. In the garage is a large, new Dodge. The motor looks like it has hardly been used. We inquire as to whether the car is roadworthy. We all have the same thought—to seize it for our continued travel northward. In the doorframe we read a little sign in Norwegian, *Strømmen Verksted, Oslo* (Strømmen Workshop, an automobile assembly plant in Norway). How wonderful! But unfortunately, the car isn't drivable.

In our crowded Opel we drive on without stopping and reach Flensburg in northern Germany. We are well received by the Danish consul in the city. He stamps our exit visas with a visa to Denmark and says that it is a special joy to be able to help us on May 17.

"Welcome to Denmark," says the consul.

Then he makes a call to Padborg to notify them of our arrival. Baroness Wedell-Wedellsborg[81] who is a Red Cross representative in

81 Danish Baroness Fritze Louise Wedell-Wedellsborg (1895–1976) was an activist

Padborg crosses the border with her elegant car and driver to get us six Norwegians. Passing the border, we see German Wehrmacht soldiers dragging themselves to the ruins of the Third Reich. We rejoice and think about the old saying: The higher you fly, the harder you fall.

It is a gorgeous afternoon when we cross the border to Free Denmark on May 17. The sun is shining from a cloudless sky. The blue and white lilac bushes wave to us in the spring breeze and send delightful whiffs of spring and freedom over the countryside. It is moving to be greeted by the Danes' cordiality. The border patrols actually forget to look at our papers. They just welcome us to freedom, and overwhelm us with goodies and warm joy.

We are out of Germany. The baroness drives us to a guesthouse. It is set up for a party—for us. There is no end to all the good food the Danes serve us. Assor Hirsch, previously a competent pianist, sits down at the piano and with stiff fingers, plays the Norwegian national anthem. We sing with trembling voices and tears of joy running down our cheeks. It is a fantastic evening in a happy, free Denmark—moving, memorable, and liberatingly beautiful. We say to each other that this May 17 will surely be the most important celebration of our national holiday in our lives. At night I lie between white sheets for the first time in three years, and still can't sleep. I am far too wound up, happy, and grateful. The warm spring night streams in through the open window and lies over me.

The next day our travels take us to a refugee camp nearby. Here the Red Cross is involved in aiding prisoners to return home. For the first time we see the "White Buses." They have come to take us to Copenhagen, together with Danish police officers who are also former prisoners of the Nazis. It is a triumphant trip through a flowering Denmark decorated with flags. In city after city we are greeted with cheering. There is no end to the scenes of joy. The meals

of the Danish aid to Finland during the 1939–1940 "Winter War" with the Soviet Union and became a Danish Red Cross organizer. From late 1944 onward, she was leader of the aid office and quarantine station at Padborg on the Danish–German border where survivors from Nazi concentration camps were received after their evacuation by the Danish and Swedish Red Cross.

are overwhelming. We receive gifts. It is almost too much, both for our stomachs and our emotions. Tears flow easily. Our feelings that have been repressed for years have latitude again. A warm hug from a stranger causes our bodies to tremble in joy. A little wildflower has never been as beautiful as when a small child's hand lifts it to me and the child says, "Welcome home!" Never before has Denmark been so dear and beautiful to me as it is now.

In Copenhagen we are lodged in Frederiksberg Hospital, in our own unit. Flowers from unknown people stream in to us while we are checked for various illnesses. Leo Eitinger asks the doctors to take an extra look at me after all the illnesses I have contracted. Unbelievably, the doctors find that both my heart and lungs are healthy. My gratitude knows no bounds.

We are visited by the Red Cross ladies, Mrs. Lund and Norwegian born Borghild Hammerich,[82] married to Rear Admiral Carl Hammerich. These two women also show us humane warmth, speaking with us, letting us cry and laugh, and helping us get in touch with relatives. Sammy speaks with his father in Stockholm. Through him I send a message to my cousin Isak Mendelsohn,[83] Josef's brother,

82 Borghild Hammerich, née Schmidt (1901–1978). During World War II, she organized substantial aid from Denmark to Norway, channeling large quantities of food parcels around the nazified Norwegian authorities for the benefit of war-stricken cities, political prisoners, and the resistance movement. With her husband, Danish Rear Admiral Carl Hammerich (1888–1945), who died at the German Gestapo headquarters of Copenhagen, she initiated what became known as the Danish/Swedish Red Cross "White Buses" operation. From December 1944, this operation ensured the evacuation of Scandinavian prisoners from German concentration camps and prisons as well as tens of thousands of non-Scandinavians who were brought to Sweden for rehabilitation at the end of the war. She was the first general secretary of the Foundation for Danish–Norwegian Cooperation (1946–1978).

83 Isak Mendelsohn (1900–1973), was the eldest son of Aron Mendelsohn and Thora, née Paltiel. He was able to avoid arrest in the fall of 1941 and made it across the border to Sweden, soon followed by his wife, Ester, their daughters Rita and Berit, and their grandchildren. The family returned to Trondheim in early summer 1945 where Isak reestablished the family clothing factory, Trokofa, which eventually became one of the largest companies in the city.

who works in the office for refugees in the Swedish capital, telling him that I am alive.

We five Jews are invited to an interview in the editorial offices of the newspaper, *Politiken,*[84] at the Copenhagen town hall square. The journalist writes an article about us and our return home. Now we hear that of Denmark's 7,500 Jews, only 482 were sent to Germany. Fifty-two of them died there, primarily of natural causes.[85] The rest returned home from Theresienstadt on April 15 on the "White Buses."

Julius Paltiel with Assor and Pelle Hirsch. This photo was taken by the Danish newspaper *Politiken*. Courtesy of the Jewish Museum, Trondheim.

84 *Politiken*, Denmark's leading omnibus newspaper was founded in 1884. Until 1970, it was the main newspaper of Det Radikale Venstre (the Social Liberal Party).

85 There has been much confusion in earlier literature about the numbers of Jewish deportees from Denmark in Theresienstadt. According to Silvia Goldbaum Tarabini Fracapane, *The Jews of Denmark in the Holocaust. Life and Death in Theresienstadt Ghetto* (Abingdon: Routledge, 2021), 470 Danish Jews were deported to Theresienstadt. Five were returned shortly upon their arrival at the ghetto, and two

The day after the interview appeared in the newspaper, I receive a telegram from Trondheim:

> Julius Paltiel (Norwegian Jew) c/o *Politiken*, Copenhagen
> Happy to hear from you contact us by telephone immediately call person-to-person collect to 6621
> Karl Lagerquist

At home in Trondheim, if they are happy to hear that I am alive, they can't possibly imagine how happy I am to hear from them. I call, and we have a good conversation. The lump in my throat is so big that I almost can't get the words out. Suddenly the longing for home tears through me. It is enormous, overriding everything else. After the conversation, I need to be alone for a while. I am trembling after hearing Karl's calm and warm voice. It is good to know that he is there with all his strength and helpfulness.

We are all declared fit and get pocket money from the Red Cross. Now we can go on short trips in the city to enjoy our freedom. Each time we enter a restaurant or café, we are recognized from the picture in the paper. We are simply not allowed to pay for food or drink. Everyone is warm and humane toward us. These are unforgettable days in a blooming, flag-decked Copenhagen.

Sven Oftedal[86] is sent from the Norwegian embassy in Stockholm to help us get home. He wants to know if there are more Norwegians in

managed to jump off a deportation train and hide while still on Danish soil. In total, fifty-one Jews who were deported from Denmark died in the ghetto, in addition to two infants who had been born in the ghetto to parents from Denmark. Most died because their medical condition could not be treated adequately in the ghetto, or of illnesses that had developed due to malnutrition, overcrowding, and poor hygiene.

86 Dr. Sven Oftedal (1905–1948) was a leading labor politician, engaged in pacifist and antifascist work. He was incarcerated in Grini concentration camp in spring 1941, rearrested in spring 1942, and deported to Sachsenhausen where he worked in the infirmary as a prisoner-physician. He was part of the group of leading Socialist politicians who came to play a key role in reestablishing Norwegian democratic life after the liberation. From 1945 until his sudden death, he was Norwegian minister of social affairs.

Germany, and we answer guiltily that we simply do not know. We ask Oftedal to get us transport home. But we don't want to travel through Sweden. If we go there first, we will be interned anew and examined for diseases. We want to go directly home. Oftedal knows that a boat is going from Copenhagen to Oslo via Århus, Jutland, with Norwegian officers who have been in German captivity. He reserves places for us as well.

We board the boat in Copenhagen. Danish freedom fighters are also on board as honor guards. They have many so-called "Danish packages" with food, which are being taken to Oslo. We meet the Norwegian officers for the first time in Århus. They receive cabins according to rank. We are just former prisoners, and placed on the lowest rung of the ladder. I talk to one of the officers, an army captain from Oslo. He asks me to give him a brief account of my experiences. We seat ourselves at a table in the lounge and I begin to talk. The captain's face becomes progressively paler as he hears about my experiences in the concentration camps. It is so different from what he and the other Norwegian soldiers had experienced in Germany.

The voices on board are enthusiastic. All are looking forward to going home. We six former, ordinary prisoners don't get cots. That luxury is only granted to officers. For the whole night, we must sit in a second-class lounge together with the Danish resistance men. The officers don't make it a secret that they expect a big reception when the boat arrives in Oslo. Before we dock, they arrange themselves by rank. We stand in rows for several hours in order to enjoy the beautiful approach through the Oslo Fjord. To see Norway again is beyond moving. The land is at its most beautiful during these May days, with blooming fields, stately trees, and light that is so coveted here in the north.

Neither honor parade, nor reception committee, awaits us. We see four figures on the dock. Sammy Steinmann sees that it is three of his friends, and Assor and Pelle Hirsch's brother, Naftali Hirsch.[87] They wave to us with a Norwegian flag, together with Augusta Helliesen[88] from the Red Cross. Sammy's friends are resistance fighters—Anders

87 Naftali "Toya" Hirsch (1910–?) Survived the war in hiding in Norway.

88 Augusta Helliesen (1906–1953) was the sister of Sigrid Helliesen Lund (1892–1987), a key person in the aid of Norwegian Jews.

Holm, Per Christensen, and Karl Rønneberg. They have come to welcome us Jews home. Naftali has a small, silver cup, decorated with Norwegian flags and engraved with the text, "Buchenwald 1942–1945. Welcome to Norway. May 1945. Naftali Hirsch."

TWO

To place our feet on Norwegian soil is a wondrous experience. Norway—Norway, it sings inside of me. My legs move lightly down the ladder and onto the dock. Then heavy thoughts emerge. What am I coming home to? Nothing. An amputated youth. My loved ones no longer alive. Despite these heavy thoughts, happiness still reigns. I am free, and almost home.

Augusta Helliesen takes us to Marienlyst, where the Red Cross has established a provisional infirmary. Our homecoming is registered there. We are not military, so our papers are just stamped in Norway. No one has been waiting for us here, and there is no public assistance for continued travel home or for a stay in Oslo. Sammy goes home with one of his friends to Nordstrand, and then on to his father in Stockholm. Leo travels to friends. Alf Knudsen goes home to Lillesand. Assor, Pelle, and I remain without housing or money for food. How will we get to Trondheim?

Luckily, we have Naftali Hirsch, who takes us to an old friend from Trondheim, Kjell Wirum, who opens his home to us. It is wonderful to wander around Oslo on these happy days, but we really want to go back to Trondheim. We begin each day by checking the state railway office in the Freemasons' Lodge near the parliament. After some days we are allocated a place on the northbound train. We sit for twelve hours looking forward to returning home, but also with a strong sense of sadness in our hearts. We know that nothing will be the same.

Finally, the train rolls into the station. I press my nose against the window. Then I hang out of the window, wave excitedly, and search for familiar faces. The station is like an anthill of people with hope in their eyes. Has a family member, a dear one, a friend, or acquaintance come home with the train—one who is not known to be alive?

Several of my friends had received notice that I was coming home on that day and they are waiting for me. It is good to see their dear faces again. Karl Lagerquist is the first who embraces me with a warm, welcoming hug, then his wife, Gunvor, and my good childhood friend Bjørn Trønsdal and his parents. It is a good homecoming. They all want me to come home with them. I feel safe to be in Trondheim.

My first wish is to go home at once to Brattørgaten, but I hear that strangers are living there. Gunvor and Karl have also been thrown out of their home and have been sharing two rooms with Gunvor's mother at the home of the teacher, Ingulf Qvam.[89] So Gunvor, Karl, and I take the trolley to 27 Strindveien in the neighborhood of Singsaker. Their warm hearts do a world of good, but there is no space for me to sleep in the small two-room apartment. I get a tiny room in the attic.

During one of the first nights I'm overwhelmed by fear. Karl hears my restless steps and brings me down into the apartment. We talk for hours and eventually, he tells me to sleep in the bed between him and Gunvor. At last, I calm down. All the others have someone and it now really dawns on me that I am totally alone. The Lagerquist family and Trønsdal are the closest people to me in this initial, difficult time.

Strangers still live in the apartment on Brattørgaten. Paul Schäffer, who owned the restaurant Deutsches Haus[90] lives in my house. After a while he is forced to move. The apartment has already been cleared of everything Mamma and Pappa owned. I know that Mamma took some silverware to one of the city's goldsmiths for safekeeping. When I go to get it, I hear the silver has been melted. The goldsmith didn't dare to keep it because the silver was engraved with the initial "P"! He offered me some plain silver, but I refused. What I really wanted was gone; some physical memento of my parents and life from before the war.

89 Ingulf Hafslo Qvam (1870–1955) was a teacher at the Trondheim Katedralskole (high school).

90 Ever since its construction in 1900, the Masonic Lodge on Kongens gate 3 was Trondheim's main concbert hall. During the occupation, the Germans took over the building as a leisure facility.

Our men's clothing business had been founded in 1891 and had become one of the largest stores of its kind in Trondheim. The Norwegian government confiscated the business at the same time as my mother was taken away in October 1942. They ran the shop until 1945 when the war caused such severe shortages that there were no longer enough wares to be sold. When the government could no longer profit from operating the store, they rented the business premises to Stranger-Thorsen, who was a building contractor working for the Germans and had an Oslo-based firm. I go to our store, which is totally destroyed and completely empty aside from a few shelves. My mood changes, and pain lies deep within me when I visit Brattørgaten. Even if the facade is the same, everything else is different.

The local newspaper, *Addresseavisen*, has written that Assor, Pelle, and I have come home to Trondheim, and two of Mamma's friends from out of town call me. They tell me that Mamma left some envelopes in their charge. The envelopes contain a few thousand kroner, which is quite helpful to me. That is all that's left. But it doesn't matter. Material things are not important and can be acquired again. The only important thing is that I am alive!

Trondheim is so beautiful. I dreamed about this night after night in the hell of the concentration camps. I walk around the streets, feel the earth under my feet, and smell the fresh breeze from the canal. My blood rushes through my veins as I slowly take in my hometown again. It's almost as if the statue of the city founder, Olav Tryggvason, is smiling down on me, on Torvet (the city square), where fruit and vegetable peddlers hawk their wares and colorful flowers. The stores are unpleasantly empty, but the Norwegian flag and pictures of the king decorate almost every window. The people are smiling and are happy.

But loneliness doesn't allow itself to be repressed. It almost knocks me out. To whom can I speak about my experiences? Who can bear to hear about the evil? No one can understand what I have seen, and I can't bear to tell it either. Many old friends come to the Lagerquists' apartment to greet me. Gunvor is kept busy with serving substitute coffee and getting ration cards so she can offer my guests baked goods.

The bright summer days are full of emptiness, though. I turn twenty-one that summer. I can finally take over my family's old apartment on Brattørgaten. Not a stick of furniture remains. Everything is gone. Nights are the worst, sitting alone on a simple chair in the home that was once so full of life and happy voices. I stand next to the window for many long night hours and dream myself back to happier times. When I look out over the fjord, I am back in the land of my childhood. I have many questions. Why were the Jews persecuted and mass murdered? What happened to the God of my childhood? Doesn't He exist? If there is a God, why did He let this happen? I can't accept that some sort of good power is guiding us. I have seen too much evil.

There is a lot to be rebuilt. I must learn to find a way back to everyday life. But what is "everyday?" After all these months and years of imprisonment, "everyday" doesn't exist any longer. I am full of pain and bitterness over what has happened. But friends support me. We speak about the years that have passed. Several of them were members of the resistance and saw brutality become part of the system. They have been through a lot, but believe the sacrifice has not been too great for a free Norway.

My old friend Sten Stensrud[91] comes one day and asks me to come home with him to visit his sick father. Before the war I went to the family's home on their farm daily, so I therefore look forward to visit Sten's family again. His father gives me a warm welcome and tells me that all through the war he was certain that I would return. He was just as certain that his own sons would survive: Per,[92] who was interned in German jails in Norway several times; and Thore,[93] who was a fighter

91 Sten Stensrud (1925–2008) was the son of Kristoffer Niels Stensrud (1884–1946) and Ingeborg, née Thue (1889–1984), who owned the large Britannia Hotel in Trondheim. From 1951 onward, he joined his mother in managing the hotel, which had been appropriated by the Germans and was slowly being restored to its former splendor.

92 Per Kristofferson Stensrud (1915–1993) was an engineer from the Norwegian Institute of Technology in Oslo and took part in the resistance as a member of the Milorg 11 group. He was arrested, tortured, and incarcerated in several Norwegian prisons and camps.

93 Thore Kristoffer Stensrud (1919–1999) served as a pilot in the Norwegian Royal Navy Airforce, which trained in Canada and flew missions to the Norwegian coast from Scotland and England.

pilot in the Norwegian Royal Navy Airforce. Most importantly, said the aging man, was that the household's loyal housekeeper, Fina, had prayed for all three of us every single day.

During the nights, I am alone. No one can help me when nightmares send me back to life in the camp. The pressure settles in my head as if pressing me into the pillow. I dream that they are after me, grabbing me in a stranglehold, and I can't breathe. My heart beats frantically. I wake up and rush to the open window to get air and try to calm myself. The fear chases me into the coming years. On many occasions I walk around all night, not daring to lie down for fear of these nightmares and difficulty breathing. But really, I am lucky. My heart, lungs, and stomach function normally. In spite of everything, my body has endured the stress.

I throw myself into a life with friends, do everything possible to get into shape. I play soccer and team handball, try to fill the many hours with activities together with others. Soon I am in such good physical shape that friends in the Rapp Sports Association[94] convince me to take part in the summer soccer Peace Cup tournament. I take long walks in Bymarka, the public woods, to strengthen my muscles and enjoy the feeling of grass under the soles of my feet. My body is thriving in the outdoors.

The people who fled to Sweden return home again. A couple of my cousins had managed to survive. But of the 250 Jews who belonged to the Jewish community of Trondheim, to the local Jewish synagogue, only 120 return. Henrik Mendelsohn, my cousin and guardian who was imprisoned with me, does not come back. His widow, Ragna, is Swedish, and invites me to Uddevalla, in Sweden, to give me new clothes and fatten me up. I need time to relax; my homecoming has been an emotionally difficult time and it has taken its toll. I say yes to the opportunity to visit her and the family. With them I speak about the

94 Rapp was founded in 1898 by a group of ten-to-twelve-year-old boys. It was the first soccer club in Trondheim. Expanding its activities to include a wide range of other sports, it became the city's leading sports club. In 1940, the Germans demanded that the leadership be dismissed. As a result, the activities ceased. When it was reestablished in 1945, the organization played a leading role in the sporting life of Trondheim once again.

future. Their friendliness and warmth fill me with calm and positive thoughts and energy.

THREE

Life slowly begins to take shape. Days fall into a regular rhythm. I decide to reopen Pappa's men's clothing store. But for the time being there is nothing to sell. Karl Lagerquist and I study the firm's old protocols and write letters to all the suppliers from before the war. The response is overwhelmingly positive. It turns out that the firm will be able to get large allocations of merchandise because of the large amounts it purchased before the war. I travel to the factories and speak personally with the management. I am well received everywhere. In fact, I am given more than the quota that a firm my size should receive. Now I can use all my energy and initiative in reestablishing the family business. Now I will be able to earn an independent living.

Julius Paltiel's family clothing store, c. 1960. Courtesy of the Jewish Museum, Trondheim.

The criminal case against Vidkun Quisling[95] is being prepared. First, I am requested to make a statement to the police in Trondheim. On July 18, 1945, I accuse him of the murder of 750 Norwegian Jews. I am called in again, this time to testify at Eidsivating Regional Court in front of judges and a jury. To have to describe my time as a prisoner in the concentration camps is a heavy burden. The packed courtroom is totally quiet while I deliver my testimony.

It is the end of the summer of 1945. The fallen leaves on the soft forest floor rustle and the veil of fall has begun to color the warm sunlight, when, on August 20, I find myself in the Falstad forest. I have been asked to take part in the exhumation and identification of the bodies of Kalman Glick, Moritz Abrahamsen, and Herman Schidorsky. It is a difficult ordeal. Ljuban Vuković leads me into the Falstad forest. He wants to lead us to the burial site itself. As witnesses, my old teacher Magne Håve, police officer Ivar Grong, architect Helge Thiis, journalist Arne Aunaas, dental technician Erling Nielsen, and I will identify the corpses. We stand and watch the interned German SS soldiers and officers dig up the corpses according to Ljuban's directions.

The detestable Gestapo chief in Trondheim, Gerhard Flesch, is digging. I am overpowered by a need to kick Flesch down into the grave, where he sent so many innocent victims to their deaths. I rush forward and kick him down into the grave. A delightful feeling fills me. He looks at me stunned. His face tightens, his eyes are full of contempt. It's as if Flesch wants to say, "See, we were right, that's how the Jews are!"

The police officer Ivar Grong and one other person come forward and grab me, holding me tightly. They are surely fearful about what I may be planning to do. But Flesch deserved to be kicked. It doesn't take long before I regain control and feel myself again. Several graves turn out to be empty. Where are the corpses? Perhaps they were dug up and sunk in the Trondheim Fjord just like the ten people who were killed during the period of martial law in October 1942. What did the

95 Vidkun Quisling was sentenced to death on September 10, 1945, for high treason and executed on October 24, 1945. Among the counts were conspiracy with the Germans prior to the April 9, 1940 invasion and his responsibility for the deportation of the Jews and the murder of Norwegian resistance fighters.

Germans want to hide? The three we were searching for were not found until June 1947. Only then did they get their final resting place at the Jewish cemetery in Trondheim.

On November 5, 1946, testimony is given against Gerhard Flesch in Frostating Regional Court. Flesch disappeared from the Gestapo headquarters in the Misjonshotell in Trondheim while liberation was being celebrated in May. Later that summer he was found in a camp for Germans in Skien in southern Norway. There he posed as a noncommissioned officer called Fleischer and wore a regular German army uniform. Late in the summer he was transferred to Falstad prison camp, where Gestapo members and Nazis awaiting trial were being held.

Oberregierungsrat SS-Obersturmbannführer Gerhard Friedrich Ernst Flesch was born in 1909 and qualified as a lawyer in 1936. He was a judge for the Gestapo and was responsible for the political surveillance of religious groups. Flesch came to Norway on April 23, 1940, lived in Bergen at first, and then came to Trondheim on October 11, 1941. There, he was responsible for the central area from Nordfjord/ Dombås in the south to the Arctic Circle in the north, which he ruled with a firm hand. After the German capitulation, not a single piece of paper was found in the Misjonshotell that could serve as evidence of his crimes. Everything had been removed.

The trial began on November 4, 1946. The prosecutor is state attorney Peder Andreas Meland, the defense is supreme court lawyer Harald Holthe. During the trial, Flesch is just as arrogant as always, especially when confronted by Jewish witnesses. The newspaper *Nidaros* reported,

> We now see a totally different picture of Flesch, and it's not the one he is trying to present in court. When the persecution of Jews began, he obviously never thought that any of them would come forward as witness against him. It was clearly visible from his facial expression that he had difficulty swallowing this, and his attempt to deny the truth of the testimony was not particularly successful.[96]

96 *Nidaros,* November 7, 1946.

Flesch declares that he is still an antisemite. The accusation against Flesch includes many serious matters, many of them concerning the treatment of Jews. Mistreatment at Falstad and the liquidation of Glick, Schidorsky, and Abrahamsen are counts in the indictment. His orders to the Falstad camp commander Gneist,[97] that no sick Jews were to be admitted to the infirmary but should have graves dug for them as quickly as possible, was also a count in the formal charges.

The murder of the three Jews is one of the strongest counts of the indictment. But his encouragement of corporal punishment and abuse of Jews together with his unlimited power over, and brutal harassment of, prisoners and the civilian population in the district are strong counts in the indictment, too.

On December 2, 1946, Flesch is sentenced to death. The sentence is upheld during the appeals process in the Supreme Court. On February 28, 1947, Flesch is executed in the Kristiansten Fortress in Trondheim. Dr. Carl Viggo Lange[98] is present. He walks over to the prisoner who is tied to a pole. Dr. Lange attaches the round target on Flesch's breast. The last words Flesch utters are, "*Heil Hitler*." A volley of shots sounds. Gerhard Friedrich Ernst Flesch is dead.

97 The commandants of the Falstad camp changed frequently. At the time of the murder of the three Jewish prisoners, Hans Roth held the post—an appointment that Flesch mandated so that a harsher regime could be introduced. "Roth was among the worst when it came to brutalizing the prisoners." One eyewitness declared, "He was, even for a German officer, extremely loud in the mouth at all times and was a terror to the prisoners." A postwar court sentenced Roth to fifteen years in prison, but acquitted him of the killing of the Jewish prisoners. Gneist was an ordinary German police officer in the camp.

98 Dr. Carl Viggo Lange (1904–1999) was a Norwegian Labor politician. He was a physician in Trondheim (1934–1955) but spent 1942–1945 as a prisoner in the Falstad camp. After 1945, he was a member of the Trondheim city council and the Norwegian parliament.

AFTERWORD

In the years that have passed since the war, I have asked myself many times: Why was I allowed to live when so many died? Why were all borders closed to Jewish refugees? These questions will always stay with me.

Because the world cannot say that it didn't know. Maria-Pia Boëthius asserts that the Swedes could have done so much: "As early as August 29, 1941, Carlos Adlercreutz, the chief for the Swedish intelligence, had received the first letter from the Swedish military attaché, Curt Juhlin-Dannfelt in Berlin, about the mass murder of Jews. On April 20, 1942, Sweden got the first report about German genocidal politics and about the 'Final Solution.'"[99]

According to Henrik Dethlefsen, in December 1942, the League of Nations condemned the mass murders in Poland, as they had been reported by the BBC.[100] Many other sources had warned the Allies about what awaited the Jews in Europe. But even the Allies did not understand, or want to understand, what was about to happen. The evil

99 Maria-Pia Boëthius, *Ære og samvittighet: Sverige og forholdet til andre verdenskrig* (Oslo: Grøndahl, 1991).

100 Henrik Dethlefsen, "Ud af mørket—den danske modstand og redningen af jøderne i oktober 1943," in Hans Sode-Madsen, Bent Blüdnikow et al., *Føreren har befalet!: jødeaktionen oktober 1943* (Copenhagen: Samleren, 1993).

of man and Hitler's pathological hate of the Jews were impossible for others to comprehend. Even though it should have been possible to see where it was leading already after the "*Kristallnacht*" pogrom on November 9–10, 1938.

I have visited Auschwitz twice since I was a prisoner there. The first time was after twenty-five years, the second after fifty years. When I entered through the gate with the inscription *Arbeit macht frei*, a cold chill settled over me once more. I saw before me the grayness, heard the complaints of the prisoners, saw endless lines of broken men, heard the barking of the German shepherd dogs and the bellowing of the SS soldiers. I walked through the museum in Auschwitz and saw the mountains of eyeglasses and children's shoes on display. Thousands of children's shoes in which the feet of happy children once ran. The suitcases, shaving brushes, human hair. Floor to ceiling, wall-to-wall display cases of human hair, cut off prisoners who died in the gas chambers. All the hair is the same color, an indescribable metal-gray color. Because of the gas, I assume. Maybe it is Mamma's or another relative's hair that lies here in front of me, I think. This was my daily life for almost thirty-one months.

Then, just as now, the Nazis had followers in every country. Today we must still be on guard. We should not lay blame for that which happened on today's generation, but what happens today and in the future is its responsibility. We must stand together against all forms of racism, fascism, Nazism, antisemitism. By learning about history, we can avoid repetition. Fear will always haunt us who survived. Just under the surface there is an undetonated bomb, which wakes us in the night while sweat runs down our faces and our hearts race at a wild pace.

I met many of those who survived on June 15, 1981 in Jerusalem. A committee of surviving prisoners invited all survivors of the Holocaust to a conference in Israel. Leading this event was Ernest W. Michel from the USA. In his opening speech he said:

> We survivors want to tell those who try to rewrite history and deny that the Holocaust ever happened: Our eyes have seen; Our ears have heard.... These hands have carried more corpses than I care to remember: Friends, families. So don't tell us it never happened.

> We were there. To deny us that part of our lives negates our very existence. We are the living witnesses and we will continue to speak out until the last survivor is no more. After that, only faces on films and our recorded voices will be left to tell future generations.[101]

At the conclusion of this conference, 6,000 survivors went to the Wailing Wall in Jerusalem. Each and every one lit a candle, one candle for every thousandth victim. We held each other's hands as the shofar (ram's horn) was blown under Israel's starlit sky. We promised one another that such a tragedy must never happen again, either for the Jewish people or any other people. No more Auschwitz, Buchenwald, Treblinka, Mauthausen, Sobibor, Sachsenhausen, Ravensbrück, Theresienstadt, Dachau, Bergen-Belsen, Natzweiler, Neuengamme, Babi Yar. NEVER AGAIN!

Julius Paltiel (far left) at a memorial ceremony in Trondheim.
Photo Collection, YVA, 1062/1.

101 Sam E. Bloch, ed., *From Holocaust to Redemption: Bearing Witness. A documentary volume depicting the proceedings and events of the World Gathering of Jewish Holocaust Survivors, Israel, June 1981* (New York: The World Gathering of Jewish Holocaust Survivors, 1984), p. 50.

We decided to write this book because Nazism is again growing in Europe. We never believed that an ideology that destroyed large parts of Europe would again find a place to grow.

International sources show that neo-Nazism is also growing on the American continent. Revisionists, the historians that support the neo-Nazi movement, write long treatises that contend that the Holocaust is just Jewish propaganda. This is especially painful because of the great losses the Jewish people suffered. Six million Jews were killed, 1.5 million of them were children. We know that the revisionists' lies can be contagious, the same way that Nazism was in the 1930s and 1940s.

I experienced everything that is in this book myself. I, Julius Paltiel, was there. I saw it and physically felt it. Told accurately by Vera Komissar, this is my personal testimony of the Holocaust.

Julius Paltiel skiing, c. 1950. Courtesy of the Jewish Museum, Trondheim.